SPECIAL MESSAGE TO READERS

THE ULVERSCROFT FOUNDATION
(registered UK charity number 264873)
was established in 1972 to provide funds for research, diagnosis and treatment of eye diseases. Examples of major projects funded by the Ulverscroft Foundation are:-

- The Children's Eye Unit at Moorfields Eye Hospital, London
- The Ulverscroft Children's Eye Unit at Great Ormond Street Hospital for Sick Children
- Funding research into eye diseases and treatment at the Department of Ophthalmology, University of Leicester
- The Ulverscroft Vision Research Group, Institute of Child Health
- Twin operating theatres at the Western Ophthalmic Hospital, London
- The Chair of Ophthalmology at the Royal Australian College of Ophthalmologists

You can help further the work of the Foundation by making a donation or leaving a legacy. Every contribution is gratefully received. If you would like to help support the Foundation or require further information, please contact:

THE ULVERSCROFT FOUNDATION
The Green, Bradgate Road, Anstey
Leicester LE7 7FU, England
Tel: (0116) 236 4325

website: www.foundation.ulverscroft.com

Read the latest news and stories from James and Bob at streetcatbob.blogspot.co.uk, and at Bob's very own Twitter site: @streetcatbob

A STREET CAT NAMED BOB

When James Bowen found an injured, ginger street cat curled up in the hallway of his sheltered accommodation, he had no idea just how much his life was about to change. James was living hand to mouth on the streets of London and the last thing he needed was a pet. Yet James couldn't resist helping the strikingly intelligent tomcat, whom he christened Bob. He slowly nursed Bob back to health and then sent the cat on his way, imagining he would never see him again. But Bob had other ideas. Soon the two were inseparable and their diverse, comic and occasionally dangerous adventures would transform both their lives, slowly healing the scars of each other's troubled pasts.

JAMES BOWEN

A STREET CAT NAMED BOB

Complete and Unabridged

CHARNWOOD
Leicester

First published in Great Britain in 2012 by
Hodder & Stoughton
London

First Charnwood Edition
published 2013
by arrangement with
Hodder & Stoughton
An Hachette UK company
London

A catalogue record for this book is available
from the British Library.

ISBN 978–1–4448–1549–8

This book is printed on acid-free paper

*To Bryn Fox . . . and anyone who
has lost a friend*

Contents

1

Fellow Travellers

There's a famous quote I read somewhere. It says we are all given second chances every day of our lives. They are there for the taking, it's just that we don't usually take them.

I spent a big chunk of my life proving that quote. I was given a lot of opportunities, sometimes on a daily basis. For a long time I failed to take any of them, but then, in the early spring of 2007, that finally began to change. It was then that I befriended Bob. Looking back on it, something tells me it might have been his second chance too.

I first encountered him on a gloomy, Thursday evening in March. London hadn't quite shaken off the winter and it was still bitingly cold on the streets, especially when the winds blew in off the Thames. There had even been a hint of frost in the air that night, which was why I'd arrived back at my new, sheltered accommodation in Tottenham, north London, a little earlier than usual after a day busking around Covent Garden.

As normal, I had my black guitar case and rucksack slung over my shoulders but this evening I also had my closest friend, Belle, with me. We'd gone out together years ago but were just mates now. We were going to eat a cheap takeaway curry and watch a movie on the small black and white television set I'd managed to find in a charity shop round the corner.

As usual, the lift in the apartment block wasn't working so we headed for the first flight of stairs, resigned to making the long trudge up to the fifth floor.

The strip lighting in the hallway was broken and part of the ground floor was swathed in darkness, but as we made our way to the stairwell I couldn't help noticing a pair of glowing eyes in the gloom. When I heard a gentle, slightly plaintive meowing I realised what it was.

Edging closer, in the half-light I could see a ginger cat curled up on a doormat outside one of the ground-floor flats in the corridor that led off the hallway.

I'd grown up with cats and had always had a bit of a soft spot for them. As I moved in and got a good look I could tell he was a tom, a male.

I hadn't seen him around the flats before, but even in the darkness I could tell there was something about him, I could already tell that he had something of a personality. He wasn't in the slightest bit nervous, in fact, completely the opposite. There was a quiet, unflappable confidence about him. He looked like he was very much at home here in the shadows and to judge by the way he was fixing me with a steady, curious, intelligent stare, I was the one who was straying into his territory. It was as if he was saying: 'So who are you and what brings you here?'

I couldn't resist kneeling down and introducing myself.

'Hello, mate. I've not seen you before, do you live here?' I said.

He just looked at me with the same studious, slightly aloof expression, as if he was still weighing me up.

I decided to stroke his neck, partly to make friends but partly to see if he was wearing a collar or any form of identification. It was hard to tell in the dark, but I realised there was nothing, which immediately suggested to me that he was a stray. London had more than its fair share of those.

He seemed to be enjoying the affection, and began brushing himself lightly against me. As I petted him a little more, I could feel that his coat was in poor condition, with uneven bald patches here and there. He was clearly in need of a good meal. From the way he was rubbing against me, he was also in need of a bit of TLC.

'Poor chap, I think he's a stray. He's not got a collar and he's really thin,' I said, looking up at Belle, who was waiting patiently by the foot of the stairs.

She knew I had a weakness for cats.

'No, James, you can't have him,' she said, nodding towards the door of the flat that the cat was sitting outside. 'He can't have just wandered in here and settled on this spot, he must belong to whoever lives there. Probably waiting for them to come home and let him in.'

Reluctantly, I agreed with her. I couldn't just pick up a cat and take him home with me, even if all the signs pointed to the fact it was homeless. I'd barely moved into this place myself and was still trying to sort out my flat. What if it did belong to the person living in that flat? They weren't going to take too kindly to someone carrying off their pet, were they?

Besides, the last thing I needed right now was the extra responsibility of a cat. I was a failed musician and recovering drug addict living a hand-to-mouth existence in sheltered accommodation. Taking responsibility for myself was hard enough.

★　★　★

The following morning, Friday, I headed downstairs to find the ginger tom still sitting there. It was as if he hadn't shifted from the same spot in the past twelve hours or so.

Once again I dropped down on one knee and stroked him. Once again it was obvious that he loved it. He was purring away, appreciating the attention he was getting. He hadn't learned to trust me 100 per cent yet. But I could tell he thought I was OK.

In the daylight I could see that he was a gorgeous creature. He had a really striking face with amazingly piercing green eyes, although, looking closer, I could tell that he must have been in a fight or an accident because there were scratches on his face and legs. As I'd guessed the previous evening, his coat was in very poor condition. It was very thin and wiry in places with at least half a dozen bald patches where you could see the skin. I was now feeling genuinely concerned about him, but again I told myself that I had more than enough to worry about getting myself straightened out. So, more than a little reluctantly, I headed off to catch the bus from Tottenham to central London and Covent Garden where I was going to once more try and earn a few quid busking.

By the time I got back that night it was pretty late, almost ten o'clock. I immediately headed for the corridor where I'd seen the ginger tom but there was no sign of him. Part of me was disappointed. I'd taken a bit of a shine to him. But mostly I felt relieved. I assumed he must have been let in by his owner when they'd got back from wherever it was they had been.

★   ★   ★

My heart sank a bit when I went down again the next day and saw him back in the same position again. By now he was slightly more vulnerable and dishevelled than before. He looked cold and hungry and he was shaking a little.

'Still here then,' I said, stroking him. 'Not looking so good today.'

I decided that this had gone on for long enough.

So I knocked on the door of the flat. I felt I had to say something. If this was their pet, it was no way to treat him. He needed something to eat and drink — and maybe even some medical attention.

A guy appeared at the door. He was unshaven,

5

wearing a T-shirt and a pair of tracksuit bottoms and looked like he'd been sleeping even though it was the middle of the afternoon.

'Sorry to bother you, mate. Is this your cat?' I asked him.

For a second he looked at me as if I was slightly mad.

'What cat?' he said, before looking down and seeing the ginger tom curled up in a ball on the doormat.

'Oh. No,' he said, with a disinterested shrug. 'Nothing to do with me, mate.'

'He's been there for days,' I said, again drawing a blank look.

'Has he? Must have smelled cooking or something. Well, as I say, nothing to do with me.'

He then slammed the door shut.

I made my mind up immediately.

'OK, mate, you are coming with me,' I said, digging into my rucksack for the box of biscuits I carried specifically to give treats to the cats and dogs that regularly approached me when I was busking.

I rattled it at him and he was immediately up on all fours, following me.

I could see he was a bit uneasy on his feet and was carrying one of his back legs in an awkward manner, so we took our time climbing the five flights of stairs. A few minutes later we were safely ensconced in my flat.

My flat was threadbare, it's fair to say. Apart from the telly, all I had in there was a second-hand sofa bed, a mattress in the corner of the small bedroom, and in the kitchen area a half-working refrigerator, a microwave, a kettle and a toaster. There was no cooker. The only other things in the flat were my books, videos and knick-knacks.

I'm a bit of a magpie; I collect all sorts of stuff from the street. At that time I had a broken parking meter in one corner, and a broken mannequin with a cowboy hat on its head in another. A friend once called my place 'the old curiosity shop', but as he sussed out his new environment the only thing the tom was curious about was the kitchen.

I fished out some milk from the fridge, poured it into a saucer and mixed it with a bit of water. I know that — contrary to popular opinion — milk can be bad for cats because, in fact, they are actually lactose intolerant. He lapped it up in seconds.

I had a bit of tuna in the fridge so I mixed it up with some mashed up biscuits and gave that to him as well. Again, he wolfed it down. *Poor thing, he must be absolutely starving*, I thought to myself.

After the cold and dark of the corridor, the flat was five-star luxury as far as the tom was concerned. He seemed very pleased to be there and after being fed in the kitchen he headed for the living room where he curled up on the floor, near the radiator.

As I sat and watched him more carefully, there was no doubt in my mind that there was something wrong with his leg. Sure enough, when I sat on the floor next to him and started examining him I found that he had a big abscess on the back of his rear right leg. The wound was the size of a large, canine-like tooth, which gave me a good idea how he'd got it. He'd probably been attacked by a dog, or possibly a fox, that had stuck its teeth into his leg and clung on to him as he'd tried to escape. He also had a lot of scratches, one on his face not far from his eye, and others on his coat and legs.

I sterilised the wound as best as I could by putting him in the bathtub then putting some non-alcoholic moisturiser around the wound and some Vaseline on the wound itself. A lot of cats would have created havoc if I'd tried to treat them like that but he was as good as gold.

He spent most of the rest of the day curled up on what was already his favourite spot, near the radiator. But he also roamed around the flat a bit every now and again, jumping up and scratching at whatever he could find. Having ignored it earlier on, he now began to find the mannequin in the corner a bit of a magnet. I didn't mind. He could do whatever he liked to it.

I knew ginger toms could be very lively and could tell he had a lot of pent-up energy. When I went to stroke him, he jumped up and started pawing at me. At one point he got quite animated, scratching furiously and almost cutting my hand

'OK, mate, calm down,' I said, lifting him off me and putting him down on the floor. I knew that young males who hadn't been neutered could become extremely lively. My guess was that he was still 'complete' and was well into puberty. I couldn't be sure, of course, but it again underlined the nagging feeling that he must have come off the streets rather than from a home.

I spent the evening watching television, the tom curled up by the radiator, seemingly content to be there. He only moved when I went to bed, picking himself up and following me into the bedroom where he wrapped himself up into a ball by my feet at the edge of the bed.

As I listened to his gentle purring in the dark, it felt good to have him there. He was company, I guess. I'd not had a lot of that lately.

★   ★   ★

On Sunday morning I got up reasonably early and decided to hit the streets to see if I could find his owner. I figured that someone might have stuck up a 'Lost Cat' poster. There was almost always a photocopied appeal for the return of a missing pet plastered on local lamp-posts, noticeboards and even bus stops. There seemed to be so many missing moggies that there were times when I wondered whether there was a cat-napping gang at work in the area.

Just in case I found the owner quickly, I took the cat with me, attaching him to a leash I'd made out of a shoelace to keep him safe. He was happy to walk by my side as we took the stairs to the ground floor.

Outside the block of flats the cat began pulling on the string lead as if he wanted to head off. I guessed that he wanted to do his business. Sure enough he headed off into a patch of greenery and bushes adjoining a neighbouring building and disappeared for a minute or two to heed nature's call. He then returned to me and happily slipped back into the lead.

He must really trust me, I thought to myself. I immediately felt that I had to repay that trust and try and help him out.

My first port of call was the lady who lived across the street. She was known locally for looking after cats. She fed the neighbourhood strays and got them neutered, if necessary. When she opened the door I saw at least five cats living inside. Goodness knows how many more she had out the back. It seemed that every cat for miles headed to her backyard knowing it was the best place to get some food. I didn't know how she could afford to feed them all.

She saw the tom and took a shine to him straight away, offering him a little treat.

She was a lovely lady but didn't know anything about where he'd come from. She'd not seen him around the area.

'I bet he's come from somewhere else in London. Wouldn't surprise me if he's been dumped,' she said. She said she'd keep her eyes and ears open in case she heard anything.

I had a feeling she was right about him being from somewhere far from Tottenham.

Out of interest, I took the cat off his lead to see if he knew what direction to go in. But as we walked the streets, it was obvious he didn't know where he was. He seemed completely lost. He looked at me as if to say: 'I don't know where I am; I want to stay with you.'

We were out for a few hours. At one point he scurried off into a bush to do his business again, leaving me to ask any passing locals whether they recognised him. All I got was blank looks and shrugs.

It was obvious that he didn't want to leave me. As we wandered around, I couldn't help wondering about his story: where he'd come from and what sort of life he'd led before he'd come and sat on the mat downstairs.

Part of me was convinced that the 'cat lady' across the street was right and he was a family pet. He was a fine-looking cat and had probably been bought for Christmas or someone's birthday. Gingers can be a bit mental and worse if not neutered, as I'd already seen. They can get very dominant, much more so than other cats. My hunch was that when he'd become boisterous and frisky he had also become a little too much to handle.

I imagined the parents saying 'enough is enough' and — rather than taking him to a refuge or the RSPCA — sticking him in the back of the family car, taking him for a drive and throwing him out into the street or on to the roadside.

Cats have a great sense of direction, but he'd obviously been let loose far from home and hadn't gone back. Or maybe he'd known that it wasn't really home at all and decided to find a new one.

My other theory was that he'd belonged to an old person who had passed away.

Of course, it was possible that wasn't the case

at all. The fact that he wasn't house-trained was the main argument against him having been domesticated. But the more I got to know him the more convinced I was that he had definitely been used to being around one person. He seemed to latch on to people whom he thought would look after him. That's what he'd done with me.

The biggest clue about his background was his injury, which looked nasty. He'd definitely picked that up in a fight. From the way it was leaking pus, the wound must have been a few days old, maybe even a week. That suggested another possibility to me.

London has always had a large population of street cats, strays who wander the streets living off scraps and the comfort of strangers. Five or six hundred years ago, places like Gresham Street in the City, Clerkenwell Green and Drury Lane used to be known as 'cat streets' and were overrun with them. These strays are the flotsam and jetsam of the city, running around fighting for survival on a daily basis. A lot of them were like this ginger tom: slightly battered, broken creatures.

Maybe he'd spotted a kindred spirit in me.

2

Road To Recovery

I'd been around cats since I was a child and I felt like I had a pretty good understanding of them. While I was growing up my family had several Siamese and I remember that at one stage we also had a beautiful tortoiseshell cat. My memories of all of them were generally fond ones, but inevitably I suppose the one that stuck most vividly in my mind was the darkest.

I'd grown up in England and Australia and for a while we'd lived in a place called Craigie in Western Australia. While we were there we had a lovely, white fluffy kitten. I can't remember where we got it from but I have a feeling it might have been from a local farmer. Wherever it had come from, it was a terrible home. For whatever reason it hadn't been checked out medically before being handed over to us. It turned out the poor little thing was flea-ridden.

It hadn't been immediately apparent. The problem was that because the kitten had such thick white fur the fleas were festering in there and nobody knew. Fleas are parasites, of course. They draw the life out of other creatures to sustain their own. They basically drained this poor kitten of all its blood. By the time we spotted it, it was too late. My mother took it to the vet's but she was told that it had passed the point of no return. It had all sorts of infections and other problems. It died within a couple of weeks of us getting it. I was five or six at the time and was devastated — as was my mother.

I'd thought about the kitten often over the years, usually whenever I saw a white cat. But he had been on my mind a lot this weekend as I'd spent time with the tom. I could tell his coat was in a bad state. It really was threadbare in places. I had an awful feeling that it would suffer the same fate as the white kitten.

Sitting in the flat with him that Sunday evening, I made a decision: I wasn't going to let that happen. I wasn't going to assume that the care I had given him was going to make him better. I wasn't going to take anything for granted.

I had to take him to a vet. I knew my makeshift medication wasn't going to be good enough to heal the wound. But I had no idea what other underlying health issues he might have. I wasn't going to take the risk of waiting, so I decided to get up early the next morning and take him to the nearest RSPCA centre, down the other end of Seven Sisters Road towards Finsbury Park.

I set my alarm early and got up to give the cat a bowl of mashed biscuits and tuna. It was another grey morning, but I knew I couldn't use that as an excuse.

Given the state of his leg, I knew he wasn't going to be up to the ninety-minute walk, so I decided to carry him and placed him in a green recycling box. It wasn't ideal but I couldn't find anything else. No sooner had we set off than it was clear that he didn't like it. He kept moving, sticking his paw over the top of the box and attempting to climb out. So eventually I gave up.

'Come on, I'll carry you,' I said, picking him up with my spare arm while carrying the recycling box in the other. He was soon scrambling up on to my shoulders where he settled. I let him sit there while I carried the empty box with me all the way to the RSPCA centre.

Inside the centre, it was like stepping into a scene from hell. It was packed, mostly with dogs and their owners, most of whom seemed to be young teenage blokes with skinhead haircuts and aggressive tattoos. Seventy per cent of the dogs were Staffordshire Bull Terriers that had almost certainly been injured in fights with other dogs, probably for people's amusement.

People always talk about Britain as a 'nation of animal lovers'. There wasn't much love on display here, that was for sure. The way some people treat their pets really disgusts me.

The cat sat on my lap or on my shoulder. I could tell he was nervous, and I couldn't blame him. He was getting snarled at by most of the dogs in the waiting room. One or two were being held tightly on their leashes as they strained to get closer to him.

One by one, the dogs were ushered into the treatment room. Each time the nurse appeared, however, we were disappointed. In the end it took us four and a half hours to be seen.

Eventually, she said, 'Mr Bowen, the vet will see you now.'

He was a middle-aged vet. He had that kind of world-weary, seen-it-all expression you see on some people's faces. Maybe it was all the aggression I'd been surrounded by outside, but I felt on edge with him immediately.

'So what seems to be the problem?' he asked me.

I knew the guy was only doing his job, but I felt like saying, 'Well, if I knew that I wouldn't be here' but resisted the temptation.

I told him how I'd found the cat in the hallway of my building and pointed out the abscess on the back of his leg.

'OK, let's have a quick look at him,' he said.

He could tell the cat was in pain and gave him a small dose of diazepam to help relieve it. He then explained that he was going to issue a prescription for a two-week course of cat-strength amoxicillin.

'Come back and see me again if things haven't improved in a fortnight,' he said.

I thought I'd take the opportunity and ask about fleas. He had a quick look around his coat but said he could find nothing.

'But it's probably worth you giving him some tablets for that. It can be a problem in young cats,' he said.

Again, I resisted the temptation to tell him that I knew that. I watched as he wrote a prescription out for that as well.

To his credit, he also checked to see if the tom was microchipped. He wasn't, which again suggested to me he was a street cat.

'You should get that done when you have a

chance,' he said. 'I think he should also be neutered quite soon as well,' he added, handing me a brochure and a form advertising a free neutering scheme for strays. Given the way he tore around the house and was so boisterous with me I nodded in agreement with his diagnosis. 'I think that's a good idea,' I smiled, expecting him to at least ask a follow-up 'why?'

But the vet didn't seem interested. He was only concerned with tapping his notes into a computer screen and printing off the prescription. We were obviously on a production line that needed to be processed and pushed out the door ready for the next patient to come in. It wasn't his fault — it was the system.

Within a few minutes we were finished. Leaving the vet's surgery, I went up to the counter at the dispensary and handed over the prescription.

The white-coated lady there was a bit friendlier.

'He's a lovely-looking fellow,' she said. 'My mum had a ginger tom once. Best companion she ever had. Amazing temperament. Used to sit there at her feet watching the world go by. A bomb could have gone off and he wouldn't have left her.'

She punched in the details to the till and produced a bill.

'That will be twenty-two pounds please, love,' she said.

My heart sank.

'Twenty-two pounds! Really,' I said. I had just over thirty pounds in the whole world at that point.

'Afraid so, love,' the nurse said, looking

sympathetic but implacable at the same time.

I handed over the thirty pounds in cash and took the change.

It was a lot of money for me. A day's wages. But I knew I had no option: I couldn't let my new friend down.

'Looks like we're stuck with each other for the next fortnight,' I said to the tom as we headed out of the door and began the long walk back to the flat.

It was the truth. There was no way I was going to get rid of the cat for at least a fortnight, not until he completed his course of medicine. No one else was going to make sure he took his tablets and I couldn't let him out on the streets in case he picked up an infection.

I don't know why, but the responsibility of having him to look after galvanised me a little bit. I felt like I had an extra purpose in my life, something positive to do for someone — or something — other than myself.

That afternoon I headed to a local pet store and got him a couple of weeks' worth of food. I'd been given a sample of scientific formula food at the RSPCA and tried it on him the previous night. He'd liked it so I bought a bag of that. I also got him a supply of cat food. It cost me around nine pounds, which really was the last money I had.

That night I had to leave him on his own and head to Covent Garden with my guitar. I now had two mouths to feed.

★ ★ ★

Over the course of the next few days, as I nursed him back to health, I got to know him a little better. By now I'd given him a name: Bob. I got the idea while watching a DVD of one of my old favourite TV series, *Twin Peaks*. There was a character in that called Killer Bob. He was actually schizophrenic, a kind of Jekyll and Hyde character. Part of the time he would be a normal, sane guy, the next he would be kind of crazy and out of control. The tom was a bit like that. When he was happy and content you couldn't have wished to see a calmer, kinder cat. But when the mood took him he could be an absolute maniac, charging around the flat. I was talking to my friend Belle one night when it dawned on me.

'He's a bit like Killer Bob in *Twin Peaks*,' I said, drawing a blank look from her.

But it didn't matter. Bob it was.

It was pretty clear to me now that Bob must have lived outdoors. When it came to toilet time, he absolutely refused to go in the litter tray that I'd bought for him. Instead I had to take him downstairs and let him do his business in the gardens that surrounded the flats. He'd dash off into a bit of overgrowth and do whatever was needed then scratch up the ground to cover up the evidence.

Watching him going through his ritual one morning, I wondered whether he'd belonged to travellers. There were quite a few of them around the Tottenham area. In fact, there was a camp of them on some land near my block of flats. Maybe he'd been part of a travelling family and had somehow got left behind when they moved on. He was definitely not a house cat, that much I knew now.

There was no doubt that he was forming an affection for me. As, indeed, I was for him. At first he had been affectionate, but still a bit wary of me. But as the days passed he became more and more confident — and friendly. He could still be very boisterous and even aggressive at times. But by now I knew that was down to the fact that he needed to be neutered.

Our life settled into a bit of a routine. I'd leave Bob in the flat in the morning and head to Covent Garden where I'd play until I got enough cash. When I got home he'd be waiting for me at the front door. He would then follow me to the sofa in the front room and watch telly with me.

By now I was beginning to realise what a smart cat he was. I could see that he understood everything I was saying to him.

When I patted the sofa and invited him to come and sit next to me he did. He also knew what I meant when I told him it was time for him to have his meds. Each time he would look at me as if to say 'Do I have to?' But he wouldn't struggle while I put tablets in his mouth and rubbed his throat gently until he swallowed it. Most cats would go mad if you try to open their mouths. But he already trusted me.

It was around that point I began to realise there was something rather special about him. I'd certainly never encountered a cat quite like Bob.

He wasn't perfect, by any means. He knew

where the food lived and would regularly crash around the kitchen, knocking over pots and pans as he searched for food. The cupboards and fridge door already bore scratch marks from where he'd been frantically trying to get access to something tasty to eat.

To be fair to him, he listened if I said no.

All I had to do was say, 'No, get away from there, Bob,' and he'd slink off. Again it showed how intelligent he was. And again it raised all sorts of questions about his background. Would a feral or a street cat pay attention to what a human told them in that way? I doubted it.

I really enjoyed Bob's company but I knew I had to be careful. I couldn't form too strong a friendship because sooner or later he would want to return to the streets. He wasn't the sort of cat that was going to enjoy being cooped up permanently. He wasn't a house cat.

For the short term, however, I was his guardian and I was determined to try and fulfil that role to the best of my ability. I knew I needed to do all I could to prepare him for his return to the streets, so one morning I filled in the form the RSPCA vet had given me for the free neutering service. I stuck it in the post and, to my mild amazement, got a reply within a couple of days. The letter contained a certificate entitling us to a free neutering.

★   ★   ★

The next morning I took Bob down to do his business outside again. The litter trays I'd

21

bought him remained unsoiled and unused. He just didn't like them.

He headed for the same spot in the bushes adjoining the neighbouring houses. It seemed to be a favourite area for some reason. I suspected it was something to do with him marking his territory, something I'd read about in a science article somewhere.

As usual, he was in there for a minute or two then spent some time afterwards clearing up after him. The cleanliness and tidiness of cats never ceases to amaze me. Why was it so important to them?

He had satisfied himself that everything was right and was making his way out when he suddenly froze and tensed up, as if he'd seen something. I was about to go over to see what was bothering him when it became quite obvious what it was.

All of a sudden, Bob lunged forward at lightning speed. It really did all happen in a blur. Before I knew it, Bob had grabbed at something in the grass near the hedge. I moved in to take a closer look and saw that it was a little grey mouse, no more than three inches long.

The little fellow had clearly been trying to scurry past him but hadn't stood a chance. Bob had pounced with lightning speed and precision and now had the creature clamped between his teeth. It wasn't the prettiest of sights. The mouse's legs were thrashing around and Bob was carefully repositioning its body in his teeth so that he could finish off the mouse. It wasn't long before the inevitable happened and the little creature gave up the fight. It was at that point that Bob released it from his mouth and laid it on the ground.

I knew what was likely to happen next but I didn't want Bob to eat it. Mice were notorious breeding grounds for disease. So I knelt down and attempted to pick up his prey. He wasn't too happy about it and made a little noise that was part growl and part hiss. He then picked the mouse up again.

'Give it to me Bob,' I said, refusing to back down. 'Give it to me.'

He really wasn't too keen and this time gave me a look as if to say: 'Why should I?'

I fished around in my coat and found a nibble, offering him a trade. 'Take this instead, Bob, it will be much better for you.'

He still wasn't convinced but after a few more moments the stand-off came to a halt and he gave in. As soon as he stepped away from the mouse, I picked it up by its tail and disposed of it.

It was another reminder of what, to me anyway, is one of the many fascinating things about cats: they are lethal predators by nature. A lot of people don't like to think of their cute little kitty as a mass murderer, but that's what cats are, given half a chance. In some parts of the world, including Australia, they have strict rules on cats being let out at night because of the carnage they cause in the local bird and rodent population.

Bob had proven the point. His coolness, his speed and his skill as a killer was amazing to behold. He knew exactly what to do and how to do it.

It set me thinking again about the life he must have led before he had arrived in the hallway of the block of flats. What sort of existence had it been? Where had he lived and how had he survived? Had he relied on finding and eating prey like this every day? Had he been raised in a domestic environment or had he always lived off the land like this? How had he become the cat he was today? I would love to have known. I was sure my street cat friend had a tale or two to tell.

In many ways, this was something else that Bob and I had in common.

Ever since I'd ended up living rough on the streets, people had wondered about my past life. How had I landed myself in this position, they'd ask me? Some did it professionally, of course. I'd spoken to dozens of social workers, psychologists and even police officers who'd quizzed me about how I'd ended up living on the streets. But a lot of ordinary people would ask me about it too.

I don't know why, but people seem to be fascinated to learn how some members of society fall through the cracks. I think it's partly that feeling that 'there for the grace of God go I', that it could happen to anyone. But I think it also makes people feel better about their own lives. It makes them think, 'Well, I may think my life is bad, but it could be worse, I could be that poor sod.'

The answer to how people like me end up on the streets is always different, of course. But there are usually some similarities. Often drugs and alcohol play a big part in the story. But in an awful lot of instances, the road that led them to living on the streets stretches all the way back to their childhoods and their relationship with their family. That was certainly the way it was for me.

I lived quite a rootless childhood, mainly because I spent it travelling between the UK and Australia. I was born in Surrey but when I was three my family moved to Melbourne. My mother and father had separated by this time. While my father stayed in Surrey, my mother had got away from all the aggravation by landing a job selling for Rank Xerox, the photocopying company, in Melbourne. She was really good at it too, she was one of the company's top saleswomen.

My mother had itchy feet, however, and within about two years we had moved from Melbourne to Western Australia. We stayed there for about three or four years until I was nine or so. Life in Australia was pretty good. We lived in a succession of large bungalows, each of which had vast garden areas at the back. I had all the space a boy could want to play in and explore the world and I loved the Australian landscape. The trouble was that I didn't have any friends.

I found it very hard to fit in at school, mainly, I think, because we'd moved a lot. The chances of me settling into life in Australia disappeared when I was nine and we moved back to the UK and to Sussex, near Horsham. I enjoyed being back in England and have some happy memories of that period. I was just getting back into life in the northern hemisphere when we had to move

25

yet again — back to Western Australia, when I was around twelve.

This time we ended up in a place called Quinn's Rock. It was there that I think a lot of my problems really began. Because of all this travelling around, we never lived in one house for more than a couple of years. My mother was always buying and selling, moving all the time. I never had a family home and never grew up in one place. We were definitely living some kind of gypsy-like existence.

I'm no psychologist, although I've met my fair share of them over the years. There is no doubt in my mind that we moved home way too much, and it was not good for a growing child. It made it very hard for me to become socially adept. At school it was very hard to make friends. I was always trying too hard. I was too eager to impress, which isn't good when you are a kid. It had the opposite result: I ended up being bullied at every school I went to. It was particularly bad in Quinn's Rock.

I probably stuck out with a British accent and my eager-to-please attitude. I was a sitting target, really. One day they decided to stone me. Literally. Quinn's Rock was called Quinn's Rock for a reason and these kids took advantage of all the nice lumps of limestone that were lying around wherever you looked. I got concussion after being bombarded on the way home from school.

Things weren't helped by the fact that I didn't get on at all with my stepfather at the time, a guy called Nick. In my teenage opinion, he was a prick — and that was what I called him. Nick the Prick. My mother had met him when she joined the police back in Horsham and he had come with her out to Australia.

We continued living this same nomadic existence throughout my early teens. It was usually connected to my mother's many business ventures. She was a very successful woman. At one point she started doing telemarketing training videos. That did quite well for a while. Then she set up a woman's magazine called *City Woman*, which didn't do so well. Sometimes we'd have plenty of money and other times we'd be strapped for cash. But that never lasted for long; she was a proper entrepreneur.

By the time I was in my mid-teens I'd pretty much quit school. I left because I was just sick to death of the bullying I encountered there. I didn't get along with Nick either. And I was very independent-minded.

I became a tearaway, a wild kid who was always out late, always defying my mother and generally thumbing his nose at authority, no matter what form it took. It wasn't surprising that I had soon developed a knack for getting myself into trouble, something I have never quite shaken off.

Predictably, I got into drugs, at first sniffing glue, probably to escape from reality. I didn't get addicted to it. I only did it a couple of times after seeing another kid doing it. But it was the start of the process. After that I started smoking dope and sniffing toluene, an industrial solvent you find in nail varnish and glue. It was all

27

connected, it was all part of a cycle of behaviour, one thing led back to another, which led back to another and so on. I was angry. I felt like I hadn't had the best breaks.

Show me the child of seven and I'll show you the man, they say. I'm not so sure that you'd have spotted my future when I was seven, but you could certainly have guessed what lay ahead when I was seventeen. I was set on the road to self-destruction.

My mother tried her hardest to get me off drugs. She could see the damage I was doing — and the even worse problems I was going to cause myself if I didn't kick the habits I was forming. She did all the things mothers do. She went through my pockets trying to find drugs and even locked me in my bedroom a few times. But the locks in our house were those ones with buttons in the middle. I learned to pick them really easily with a Bobby pin. They just popped out and I was free. I wasn't going to be hemmed in by her — or anyone else for that matter. We argued even more then, of course, and inevitably things went from bad to worse. Mum got me to go to a psychiatrist at one point. They diagnosed me with everything from schizophrenia, to manic depression to ADHD, or Attention Deficit Hyperactivity Disorder. Of course, I thought it was all bullshit. I was a messed-up teenager who thought he knew better than everyone. With the benefit of hindsight I can see that my mother must have been worried sick. She must have felt powerless and terrified of what was going to happen to me. But I was oblivious to other people's feelings. I didn't care and I didn't listen to anyone.

The situation got so bad between us that for a while I lived in Christian charity accommodation. I just passed my time away there, taking drugs and playing guitar. Not necessarily in that order.

Around my eighteenth birthday, I announced that I was going to move back to London to live with my half-sister from my father's previous marriage. It marked the beginning of the downward spiral.

At the time, it had seemed like I was setting out into the world like any normal teenager. My mother had taken me to the airport and dropped me off in the car. We'd come to a stop at a red light and I'd jumped out giving her a peck on the cheek and a wave goodbye. We were both thinking that I'd be gone for six months or so. That was the plan. I would stay for six months, hang out with my half-sister and pursue my grand dreams of making it as a musician. But things wouldn't exactly go to plan.

At first, I went to stay with my half-sister in south London. My brother-in-law hadn't taken too kindly to my arrival. As I say, I was a rebellious teenager who dressed like a Goth and was — probably — a complete pain in the arse, especially as I wasn't contributing to the household bills.

In Australia I'd worked in IT and sold mobile phones but back in the UK I couldn't land a decent job. The first I'd been able to get had been working as a bartender. But my face hadn't fitted and they'd sacked me after using me to cover for other people's holidays during Christmas 1997. As if that wasn't bad enough, they wrote the dole office a letter saying I'd quit the job, which meant I couldn't collect the benefits I was eligible for by virtue of having been born in England.

After that I'd been even less welcome in my brother-in-law's house. Eventually, my half-sister and he had kicked me out. I had made contact with my dad and been to see him a couple of times, but it was clear we weren't going to be able to get on. We barely knew each other, so living there was out of the question. I started sleeping on friends' floors and sofas. Soon I was leading a nomadic existence, carrying my sleeping bag with me to various flats and squats around London. Then when I ran out of floors I moved to the streets.

Things headed downwards fast from there.

★ ★ ★

Living on the streets of London strips away your dignity, your identity — your everything, really. Worst of all, it strips away people's opinion of you. They see you are living on the streets and treat you as a non-person. They don't want anything to do with you. Soon you haven't got a real friend in the world. While I was sleeping rough I managed to get a job working as a kitchen porter. But they sacked me when they found out I was homeless, even though I'd done nothing wrong at work. When you are homeless you really stand very little chance.

The one thing that might have saved me was going back to Australia. I had a return ticket but lost my passport two weeks before the flight. I had no paper-work and besides I didn't have the money to get a new one. Any hope I had of getting back to my family in Australia disappeared. And so, in a way, did I.

★   ★   ★

The next phase of my life was a fog of drugs, drink, petty crime — and, well, hopelessness. It wasn't helped by the fact that I developed a heroin habit.

I took it at first simply to help me get to sleep at night on the streets. It anaesthetised me from the cold and the loneliness. It took me to another place. Unfortunately, it had also taken a hold of my soul as well. By 1998 I was totally dependent on it. I probably came close to death a few times, although, to be honest, I was so out of it at times that I had no idea.

During that period it didn't occur to me to contact anyone in my family. I had disappeared off the face of the earth — and I didn't really care. I was too wrapped up in surviving. Looking back at the time now, I can only imagine that they must have been going through hell. They must have been worried sick.

I got an inkling of the grief I was causing about a year after I had arrived in London and about nine months or so after I'd taken to the streets.

I had made contact with my father when I'd arrived in London but hadn't spoken to him in months. It was around Christmas time that I decided to give him a call. His wife — my stepmother — had answered the phone. He refused to come to the phone and kept me waiting for a few minutes, he was so angry with me.

'Where the f*** have you been? We've all been worried sick about you,' he said, when he had collected himself enough to talk to me.

I made some pathetic excuses but he just shouted at me.

He told me that my mother had been in contact with him desperately trying to find out where I was. That was a measure of how worried she'd become. The two of them never spoke. He shouted and screamed at me for fully five minutes. I realise now it was a mixture of release and anger. He had probably thought I was dead, which, in a way, I had been.

That period of my life lasted a year or so. I'd eventually been picked up off the streets by a homeless charity. I'd stayed in various shelters. Connections, just off St Martin's Lane, was one of them. I'd been sleeping rough in the market next door around that time.

I ended up on what's known as the 'vulnerable housing' list, which qualified me as a priority for sheltered accommodation. The problem was that for the best part of the next decade I ended up living in horrendous hostels, B&Bs and houses, sharing my space with heroin and crack addicts who would steal anything that wasn't nailed down. Everything I had was stolen at some point. I had to sleep with my most important possessions tucked inside my clothes. Survival was all I could think about.

Inevitably, my drug dependency got worse. By the time I was in my late twenties, my habit had got so bad I ended up in rehab. I spent a couple of months getting straightened out and was then put on a drug rehabilitation programme. For a while, the daily trip to the chemist and the fortnightly bus ride to my drug dependency unit in Camden became the focus of my life. They became an almost reflex. I'd get out of bed and go and do one or the other on auto-pilot, as if in a daze, which, if I'm honest, I often was.

I did some counselling there as well. I talked endlessly about my habit, how it had started — and how I was going to bring it to an end.

It's easy to come up with excuses for drug addiction, but I'm certain I know the reason for mine. It was pure and simple loneliness. Heroin allowed me to anaesthetise myself to my isolation, to the fact that I didn't have family or a huge circle of friends. I was on my own and, strange and unfathomable as it will seem to most people, heroin was my friend.

Deep down, however, I knew it was killing me — literally. So over a period of a few years I'd moved off heroin on to methadone, the synthetic opioid that is used as a substitute to wean morphine and heroin addicts off their habits. By the spring of 2007, the plan was that I would eventually start weaning myself off that and get completely straight.

The move to the flat in Tottenham was a key part of that process. It was an ordinary apartment block full of ordinary families. I knew I had a chance to put my life back on track there.

To help pay the rent I'd started busking in Covent Garden. It wasn't much but it helped put food on the table and pay the gas and electricity. It also helped to keep me on an even keel. I knew it was my chance to turn the corner. And I knew I had to take it this time. If I'd been a cat, I'd have been on my ninth life.

3

The Snip

As we approached the end of Bob's second week of medication, he was looking a lot brighter. The wound at the back of his leg was healing nicely and the bald and thin patches on his coat had begun to disappear and were being replaced with new, thicker fur. He also seemed happier in his face, his eyes had a more lustrous gleam to them. There was a beautiful, green and yellow glow to them that hadn't been there before.

He was definitely on the road to recovery, and his boisterousness around the flat was the ultimate proof of it. He had been a whirling dervish, flying around the place since day one, but in the past week or so he'd become even more of a ball of energy. I hadn't thought it possible. There were times when he would jump and run around the place like some kind of maniac. He would claw furiously at everything and anything he could find, including me.

There were scratches on every wooden surface in the flat. I even had scratches on the back of my hand and arm. I didn't mind, I knew it wasn't malicious and that he was only playing.

He had become such a menace in the kitchen, where he would claw at the cupboards and fridge door in an attempt to break into my food supplies, that I'd had to buy a couple of cheap plastic child-locks.

I also had to be careful about leaving anything lying around that might become a plaything for him. A pair of shoes or item of clothing could be scratched to bits within minutes.

All Bob's actions showed that there was something that needed to be done. I'd been around enough cats in my life to recognise the tell-tale signs. He was a young male with way too much testosterone flying around his body. There was no doubt in my mind that he needed neutering. So a couple of days before his course of medicine finished I decided to call the local vets, the Abbey Clinic on Dalston Lane.

I knew the pros and cons of keeping him 'entire', and they were mostly cons. If I didn't castrate him there would be times when Bob's hormones would completely take over and he just wouldn't be able to stop himself from roaming the streets in search of willing females. It could mean that he would go missing for days — even weeks — at a time. He'd also be far more likely to get run over and to get into fights with other cats. As far as I knew, that might have been the cause of the fight that had caused his injury. Male toms are very protective of their territory and produce a distinctive odour to signal their 'patch'. Bob might have wandered into someone else's territory and paid the price. I knew it was probably paranoia on my part, but there was also a risk, albeit a very small one, of him contracting diseases like FeLV and FIV, the feline equivalent of HIV, if he wasn't neutered.

Last, but far from least, if he stayed with me, he would also be a much calmer, more even-tempered pet. He wouldn't be so prone to running around like a maniac all the time.

By contrast the pros in favour of doing nothing amounted to a very short list. It would avoid him having to undergo a small bit of surgery. That was about it.

It was a no-brainer.

I rang the vets' surgery and spoke to a female nurse.

I explained my situation and asked whether he was eligible for a free operation. She said yes provided I had a certificate from a vet, which I did after my first visits to sort out his leg and get his flea and worm medications.

The only thing that worried me was the medication he was still taking. I explained that he was coming to the end of a course of antibiotics but she said that shouldn't be a problem. She recommended that I book him in for an operation in two days' time.

'Just bring him in and leave him with us in the morning. If everything goes to plan, you'll be able to pick him up at the end of the day,' she said.

I got up nice and early on the day of the operation, knowing that I had to get him into the surgery by 10a.m. It was the first time that we'd travelled any distance from the flat together since our visit to the RSPCA.

I hadn't let him out of the flat, apart from to do his business downstairs, because he was still on his antibiotics. So I stuck him in the same green, plastic recycling box I'd used a fortnight earlier to take him to the RSPCA. The weather was miserable so I took the lid and let it rest loosely on the box once we were out and about. He wasn't much more comfortable in it that day than he was the first time I put him in it. He kept sticking his head out and watching the world go by.

The Abbey Clinic is a small place, sandwiched between a newsagent and a medical centre on a parade of shops on Dalston Lane. We got there in plenty of time for his appointment and found the place packed. It was the usual, chaotic scene, with dogs tugging on their owners' leashes and growling at the cats inside their smart carriers. Bob stood out like a sore thumb in his impro-vised carrier so was immediately a target for their aggression. Once again, there were several Staffies there with their Neanderthal-looking owners.

Some cats would have bolted, I'm sure. But Bob wasn't fazed at all. He seemed to have placed his trust in me.

When my name was called out a young nurse in her twenties came out to meet us. She had some paperwork and led me into a room where she asked me what were obviously standard ques-tions.

'Once it's been carried out, the operation can't be reversed. So are you certain you don't want to breed from Bob at some future date?' she said.

I just smiled and nodded.

'Yeah, I'm quite certain,' I said, rubbing Bob on the head.

Her next question stumped me, however.

'And how old is Bob?' she smiled.

'Ah. I really don't know,' I said, before briefly explaining his story.

'Hmm, let's take a look.' She explained that the fact that he hadn't been neutered was a good clue about his age.

'Male and female cats tend to become sexually mature at around six months of age. If they are left 'entire' after that they go through some distinct physical changes. For instance, toms get fuller in the face, particularly around the cheeks. They also develop thicker skins and generally become quite big, certainly bigger than those cats that have been neutered,' she told me. 'He's not that big, so I'd guess that he's maybe nine to ten months old,' she said.

As she passed me the release forms, she explained that there was a minor risk of complications but that it was a really tiny chance. 'We will give him a thorough examination and maybe run a blood test before we go ahead with it,' she said. 'If there's a problem we will contact you.'

'OK,' I said, looking slightly sheepish. I didn't have a working mobile so they would have trouble contacting me.

She then took me through the procedure itself. 'The operation happens under general anaesthetic and is usually pretty straightforward. The testicles are removed through two small incisions made into the scrotal sacs.'

'Ouch, Bob,' I said giving him a playful ruffle.

'If everything goes OK, you can come and collect Bob in six hours,' she said, looking down at her watch. 'So at around four thirty. Is that OK?'

'Yeah, great,' I nodded. 'See you then.'

After giving Bob a final cuddle, I headed back out into the overcast streets. There was rain brewing once more.

I didn't have time to head all the way into central London. By the time I'd set up and sung a few songs, it would be time to turn around again. So I decided to take my chances around the nearest railway station, Dalston Kingsland. It wasn't the greatest pitch in the world, but it provided me with a few quid and a place to while away the hours as I waited for Bob. There was also a very friendly cobbler's shop next to the station where I knew I would get shelter from the inevitable rain when it came.

I tried to block Bob out of my thoughts as I played. I didn't want to think about him in the operating theatre. He had probably lived his life on the street and could well have had all sorts of other things wrong. I'd heard stories of cats and dogs going into vets' surgeries for the most minor procedures and never coming out again. I struggled to keep my darkest thoughts at bay. It didn't help that there were big black clouds glowering over me.

Time passed very, very slowly. Eventually, however, the clock reached 4.15p.m. and I began packing up. I almost ran the last few hundred yards to the clinic.

The nurse I'd seen earlier was at the reception desk talking to a colleague and greeted me with a warm smile.

'How is he? Did it all go all right?' I asked, still breathing heavily.

'He's fine, absolutely fine. Don't worry,' she said. 'Get your breath back and I'll take you through.'

It was weird, I hadn't felt this concerned about someone — or something — for years.

I went into the surgical area and saw Bob lying in a nice warm cage.

'Hello, Bob mate, how you doing?' I said.

He was still very dopey and drowsy so didn't recognise me for a while, but when he did he sat upright and started clawing at the doors of the cage as if to say: 'Let me outta here.'

The nurse got me to sign a discharge notice and then gave Bob a good once over to make sure he was fit to leave.

She was really lovely and very helpful, which made a pleasant change after the previous experience I'd had at the vets'. She showed me where the incisions had been made. 'It will stay swollen and sore around there for a couple of days, but that's normal,' she said. 'Just check every now and again to make sure there's no discharge or anything like that. If you notice that then give us a ring or bring him back in so we can check him out. I'm sure he'll be fine.'

'How long will he be groggy?' I asked her.

'Could be a couple of days before he's back to his normal bright-eyed and bushy-tailed self,' she said. 'It varies a lot, some cats bounce back immediately. With others it kind of knocks the stuffing out of them for a couple of days. But they are normally as right as rain within forty-eight hours.

'He probably won't want to eat much the day

41

after but his appetite will return fairly soon. But if he stays very sleepy and lethargic give us a ring or bring him in for a check-up. It's very rare but cats sometimes get infections from the operation,' she said.

I'd brought the recycling box along with me again, and was just about to pick Bob up to pick him up when she told me to wait.

'Hang on,' she said. 'I think we can do better than that.'

She went away for a couple of minutes and then produced a lovely, sky-blue carrying case.

'Oh, that's not mine,' I said.

'Oh, don't worry, it's OK. We've got loads of spares, you can have this one. Just drop it back in when you're next passing.'

'Really?'

I had no idea how it had got there. Maybe someone had left it behind. Or maybe someone had brought their cat in and returned to discover that it would not be needed any more. I didn't want to dwell on it too much.

It was obvious that the op had taken a lot out of Bob. In the carrier on the way home, he just lay there half asleep. The moment we got into the flat he slowly padded over to his favourite spot by the radiator and lay down. He slept there all night.

I took the day off work the next day to make sure he was OK. The advice from the vet was that he should be supervised for twenty-four to forty-eight hours after the operation to make sure there weren't any side effects. I was to particularly look out for continuing drowsiness, which wasn't a good sign. It was approaching the end of the week so I knew I'd need some money. But I could never have forgiven myself if something had gone wrong, so I stayed in the flat on twenty-four-hour Bob watch.

Fortunately, he was absolutely fine. The following morning, he was a bit perkier and ate a little bit of breakfast. As the nurse had predicted, he didn't have his normal appetite but he ate half a bowl of his favourite food, which was encouraging. He also wandered around the flat a little bit, although, again, he wasn't his normal ebullient self.

Over the next couple of days he began becoming more like the old Bob. Within three days of the op, he was wolfing down his food just like before. I could tell he was still in the occasional bit of pain. He would wince or come to a sudden stop every now and again, but it wasn't a major problem.

I knew that he'd still have the odd mad half-hour, but I was glad I'd acted.

4

Ticket To Ride

As the fortnight drew to a close, I realised that I had to think about getting Bob out of the flat and back on to the streets. That's where he had come from — and I assumed that's where he would want to return.

He'd continued to make really good progress and looked much healthier than he had done when I first met him. He'd fattened up a lot more too.

So a day or two after I'd completed the course of medicine and he'd recovered fully from his op, I took Bob downstairs and out through the hallway. I led him down the path and out towards the gate then pointed him in the direction of the street.

He just stood there, fixed to the spot, looking at me confused, as if to say: 'What do you want me to do?'

'Go, go, go on,' I said, making sweeping movements with my hands.

It had no effect whatsoever.

For a moment I just stood there, engaged in a miniature staring competition with him. But then he just turned on his heels and padded off, not in the direction of the street but towards the patch of ground where he liked to do his business. He then dug a hole, covered it all up,

44

and strolled back towards me.

This time his expression said: 'OK, I did what you wanted. What now?'

It was then that, for the first time, a thought began to crystallise in my head.

'I think you want to hang around,' I said quietly to him.

Part of me was pleased. I enjoyed his company and he was certainly a character. But, being sensible about it, I knew I shouldn't let it happen. I was still struggling to look after myself. I was still on a drug dependency programme, and would be for the foreseeable future. How on earth was I going to look after a cat, even one as intelligent and self-sufficient as Bob? It wasn't fair — on either of us.

So, with a heavy heart, I decided that I'd have to slowly start easing him out of the flat during the day. When I went to work in the morning, I would no longer leave him in the flat. I'd take him out with me, then leave him outside in the gardens.

'Tough love,' I told myself.

He didn't like it one bit.

The first time I did it, he shot me a look that said 'traitor'. As I headed off with my guitar over my shoulder, he followed, quietly stalking me, zigzagging across the pavement like some spy, trying to remain unseen. Except it was easy to spot his distinctive ginger fur, bobbing and weaving around.

Each time I saw him, I'd stop and wave my arms, flamboyantly waving him back. He'd limp away, reluctantly, throwing me a few betrayed looks as he went. Eventually he'd get the message and disappear.

When I got back six or so hours later, he would be waiting for me at the entrance to the flats. Part of me wanted to prevent him from coming in. But that part was overwhelmed by the one that wanted to invite him up to the flat once more to curl up at my feet.

Over the course of the next few days the pair of us settled into a bit of a routine.

Each day I'd leave him outside and each night when I got back from busking, I'd find him waiting for me, either outside in an alleyway or — if someone had let him in during the day — sitting on the mat outside my flat. He wasn't going away, that was obvious.

I decided I had to take the ultimate step and leave him out overnight. The first night I did it I saw him lurking in the area where the bins were kept. I tried to sneak in without him seeing me. It was a stupid move. He was a cat, he had more senses in one of his whiskers than I had in my entire body. No sooner had I opened the door to the building than he was there squeezing his way in. I left him outside in the hallway that night, but he was on my doormat when I emerged again in the morning. For the next few days we went through the same performance.

Each day I stepped outside he'd either be hanging around the hallway or would be waiting outside. Each night he'd find a way of getting into the building.

Eventually he decided that he'd won that particular battle. So I was soon dealing with another problem. He began following me down the main road.

The first time he came as far as the main road, but returned to the block when I shooed him away. The next time he tailed me for a hundred yards or so down the road, towards Tottenham High Road where I got the bus to Covent Garden.

A part of me admired his tenacity and sheer perseverance. But another part of me was cursing him. I simply couldn't shake him off.

Each day after that he got further and further — becoming bolder and bolder. Part of me wondered whether one day, after I left him, he'd actually keep going and find somewhere else to go. But each night I got home, there he was — waiting. I knew that something had to give eventually though. And it did.

★　★　★

One day I headed out for work as usual. I had packed my large black acoustic guitar with its red trim on the edge of the body, slung it over my shoulder along with my rucksack and headed downstairs.

I saw Bob was sitting in an alleyway and said hello. When he started to follow me, I shooed him away, as usual.

'Stay there, you can't come where I'm going,' I said.

This time he seemed to get the message and slunk off. As I headed down the road, I looked back occasionally to see if he was there, but there was no sign of him. *Perhaps he's finally getting the message*, I said to myself.

To get to the bus stop that would take me to Covent Garden, I had to cross Tottenham High Road, one of the busiest and most dangerous roads in north London. This morning, as usual, cars, lorries and motorbikes were carving their way along the road, trying to pick their way through the clogged traffic.

As I stood on the pavement, trying to spot a gap so that I could run for the bus that was looming into view a hundred yards or so down the traffic-packed street, I felt someone — or something — rub against my leg. Instinctively, I looked down. I saw a familiar figure standing alongside me. To my horror, I could see that Bob was going through the same process as me, looking for his opportunity to cross.

'What the hell are you doing here?' I said to him.

He just looked at me dismissively, as if I'd just asked a really stupid question. Then he focused once more on the road, nudging himself nearer the edge of the kerb as if getting ready to make a dash for it.

I couldn't let him risk it. It would almost certainly be suicide. So I swept him up and put him on my shoulder, where I knew he liked to sit. He sat there, snuggled up against the side of my head, as I sidestepped and weaved my way through the traffic and crossed the road.

'All right, Bob, that's far enough,' I said to him as I put him down on the pavement and shooed him away again.

He sidled off down the street into the throng. *Maybe now I've seen the last of him*, I thought to myself. He really was a long way from home now.

A few moments later the bus pulled up. It was an old-fashioned red double-decker bus that you could jump on at the back. I went to sit on the bench at the back of the bus and was placing my guitar case in the storage space near where the conductor was standing when, behind me, I saw a sudden flash of ginger fur. Before I knew it, Bob had jumped up and plonked himself on the seat next to where I was sitting.

I was gobsmacked. I realised — finally — that I wasn't ever going to shake this cat off. But then I realised something else.

I invited Bob to jump on my lap, which he did in the blink of an eye. A moment or two later, the conductor appeared. She was a cheerful West Indian lady and smiled at Bob, then me.

'Is he yours?' she said, stroking him.

'I guess he must be,' I said.

5

Centre of Attention

For the next forty-five minutes or so, Bob sat quietly next to me, his face pressed against the glass of the bus window, watching the world go by. He seemed to be fascinated by all the cars, cyclists, vans and pedestrians whizzing past us; he wasn't fazed at all.

The only time he pulled away from the window and looked to me for a little reassurance was when the blare of a police siren, a fire engine or an ambulance got a bit too close for comfort. This surprised me a bit and once more set me thinking about where he had spent his early life. If he had grown up on the streets he would have got used to this noise a long, long time ago.

'Nothing to worry about,' I told him, each time giving him a friendly stroke on the back of the neck. 'This is what the middle of London sounds like, Bob, better get used to it.'

It was odd, even though I knew he was a street cat and could run away at any time, I had this deep-seated feeling that he was here in my life to stay. Somehow I sensed this wouldn't be the last time we'd make this trip together.

I was going to get off at my usual bus stop near Tottenham Court Road tube station. As it loomed into view, I picked up my guitar, scooped up Bob and headed for the exit. On the pavement, I fished around in my coat pocket and found the makeshift shoelace lead that I'd left in there after taking Bob out to do his business the evening before.

I put it around his neck then placed him down. I didn't want him wandering off. The junction of Tottenham Court Road and New Oxford Street was bustling with shoppers, tourists and ordinary Londoners getting on with their day. He'd have been lost in a second — or, even worse, crushed by one of the buses or black cabs whistling towards and from Oxford Street.

Understandably, it was all a bit intimidating for Bob. It was unfamiliar territory for him — well, I assumed it was. I couldn't be sure, of course. As we picked our way along I could tell from his slightly uptight body language and the way he kept looking up at me that he was uneasy. So I decided to take one of my normal short cuts through the back streets to get to Covent Garden.

'Come on, Bob, let's get you out of the crowds,' I said.

Even then he wasn't 100 per cent happy. Weaving our way through the throng, he kept shooting me looks as if to say he wasn't quite sure about this. After only a few yards I could tell that he wanted me to pick him up.

'All right, but don't make a habit of it,' I said, gathering him up and placing him on my shoulders just as I'd done crossing Tottenham High Road. He'd soon settled into a comfortable spot, at a slight angle across my right shoulder blade, with his front paws placed on the top of my arm, looking out like the occupant of the

51

bird's nest on some pirate ship. I couldn't help smiling inwardly. I must look a bit like Long John Silver, except I had a puss rather than a parrot sailing along with me.

He certainly seemed to be very comfortable there. I could feel him purring lightly as we walked through the throng, across New Oxford Street and into the smaller streets leading down towards Covent Garden.

The crowds had thinned out by now and after a while I began to forget Bob was there. Instead I started to immerse myself in the usual thoughts that went through my mind on the way to work. Was the weather going to be good enough for me to get a solid five hours' busking? Answer: Probably. It was overcast, but the clouds were white and high in the sky. There wasn't much chance of rain. What sort of crowd would there be in Covent Garden? Well, it was getting close to Easter so there were a lot of tourists. How long would it take me to make the twenty or thirty pounds I needed to get me — and now Bob — through the next few days? Well, it had taken me the best part of five hours the previous day. Maybe it would be better today, maybe it wouldn't. That was the thing with busking; you just never knew.

I was mulling all these things over still when I was suddenly aware of something.

Ordinarily, no one would engage or even exchange a look with me. I was a busker and this was London. I didn't exist. I was a person to be avoided, shunned even. But as I walked down Neal Street that afternoon almost every person

52

we passed was looking at me. Well, more to the point, they were looking at Bob.

One or two had quizzical, slightly confused looks on their faces, which was understandable, I guess. It must have looked slightly incongruous, a tall, long-haired bloke walking along with a large, ginger tom on his shoulders. Not something you see every day — even on the streets of London.

Most people, however, were reacting more warmly. The moment they saw Bob their faces would break into broad smiles. It wasn't long before people were stopping us.

'Ah, look at you two,' said one well-dressed, middle-aged lady laden down with shopping bags. 'He's gorgeous. Can I stroke him?'

'Of course,' I said, thinking it would be a one-off event.

She plonked down her bags and placed her face right up to his.

'What a lovely fellow you are, aren't you?' she said. 'He is a boy, isn't he?'

'He is,' I said.

'Isn't he good to sit there on your shoulders like that? Don't see that very often. He must really trust you.'

I'd barely said goodbye to the lady when we were approached by two young girls. They'd seen the lady making a fuss of Bob so I guess they thought they could do the same. They turned out to be Swedish teenagers on holiday.

'What is his name? Can we take his picture?' they said, snapping away with their cameras the instant I nodded.

'His name's Bob,' I said.

'Ah, Bob. Cool.'

We chatted for a minute or two. One of them had a cat herself and produced a picture of it for me. I had to politely excuse myself after a couple of minutes, otherwise they would have spent hours drooling over him.

We carried on towards the bottom of Neal Street in the direction of Long Acre. But the going was slow. No sooner had the latest admirer gone away than the same thing was happening again — and again. I'd barely go three feet without being stopped by someone who wanted to stroke or talk to Bob.

The novelty soon wore off. At this rate I wasn't going to get anywhere, I began to realise. It normally took me not much more than ten minutes to get from my normal bus stop to my pitch at Covent Garden. But it had already taken me twice that because everyone had seemed to want to stop and talk to Bob. It was a bit ridiculous.

By the time we got to Covent Garden it was almost an hour after I normally got set up.

Thanks a lot, Bob, you've probably cost me a few quid in lost earnings, I heard myself saying in my head, half-jokingly.

It was a serious issue though. If he was going to slow me down this much every day, I really couldn't let him follow me on to the bus again, I thought. It wasn't long before I was thinking a bit differently.

★　★　★

By this point, I'd been busking around Covent Garden for about a year and a half. I generally started at about two or three in the afternoon and carried on until around eight in the evening. It was the best time to capture tourists and people finishing off their shopping or on the way home from work. At the weekends I would go earlier and do lunchtimes. On Thursday, Friday and Saturday I'd carry on until quite late, trying to take advantage of the extra numbers of Londoners that hung around at the end of the working week.

I'd learned to be flexible in finding an audience. My main pitch was on a patch of pavement directly outside Covent Garden tube station on James Street. I'd work that until about 6.30 p.m., when the main evening rush hour was at its peak. Then for the last couple of hours I'd walk around all the pubs in Covent Garden where people were standing outside smoking and drinking. In the summer months this could be quite productive as office workers unwound after their day's work with a pint and a fag in the evening sunshine.

It could be a bit risky at times. Some people took exception to me approaching them and could be rude and even abusive at times. 'Piss off you scrounger'; 'Get yourself a proper job you lazy f★★★★★.' That kind of stuff. But that came with the territory. I was used to it. There were plenty of people who were happy to hear me play a song then slip me a quid.

Busking at James Street was a bit of a gamble as well. Technically speaking, I wasn't supposed to be there.

The Covent Garden area is divided up very specifically into areas when it comes to street people. It's regulated by officials from the local council, an officious bunch that we referred to as Covent Guardians.

My pitch should have been on the eastern side of Covent Garden, near the Royal Opera House and Bow Street. That's where the musicians were supposed to operate, according to the Covent Guardians. The other side of the piazza, the western side, was where the street performers were supposed to ply their trade. The jugglers and entertainers generally pitched themselves under the balcony of the Punch and Judy pub where they usually found a rowdy audience willing to watch them.

James Street, where I had begun playing, was meant to be the domain of the human statues. There were a few of them around, one guy dressed as Charlie Chaplin used to do quite well but only worked now and again. But it was normally clear so I had taken advantage and made it my own little patch. I knew there was always the risk of getting moved along by the Covent Guardians but I took my chances and it usually paid off. The volume of people coming out of the tube station there was huge. If only one in a thousand of them made a 'drop' then I could do OK.

★ ★ ★

It was just after 3p.m. when I got to my pitch — finally. Just as we turned into James Street we

56

were stopped for the umpteenth time, on this occasion by an obviously gay guy on his way home from the gym, judging by the sweaty kit he was wearing.

He made a complete fuss of Bob and even asked me — I think jokingly — whether he could buy him off me.

'No, mate, he's not for sale,' I said politely, just in case he was serious. Walking away from the guy I just looked at Bob and shook my head. 'Only in London, mate, only in London.'

Arriving at the pitch, I firstly checked to make sure the coast was clear. There was no sign of the Covent Guardians. There were also a couple of people who worked at the tube station who sometimes gave me some hassle because they knew I wasn't supposed to be there. But they didn't seem to be around either. So I put Bob down on the pavement near the wall, unzipped my guitar case, took off my jacket and got ready to tune up.

Ordinarily it would take me a good ten minutes to get tuned, start playing and get people to pay me some attention.

Today though a couple of people slowed down in front of me and lobbed small denomination coins into my guitar case even before I'd played a note. *Generous of them*, I thought.

It was as I fiddled around, tuning my guitar, that the penny eventually dropped!

My back was turned to the crowd when I again heard the distinctive clinking of one coin hitting another. Behind me I heard a male voice. 'Nice cat, mate,' he said.

I turned and saw an ordinary-looking guy in his mid-twenties giving me a thumbs up sign and walking off with a smile on his face.

I was taken aback. Bob had curled himself up in a comfortable ball in the middle of the empty guitar case. I knew he was a charmer. But this was something else.

★ ★ ★

I'd taught myself to play the guitar when I was a teenager living back in Australia. People would show me things and then I'd work my way through them on my own. I got my first guitar when I was fifteen or sixteen. It was quite late to start playing, I suppose. I bought an old electric guitar from a Cash Converters in Melbourne. I'd always played on my friends' acoustic guitars, but I fancied an electric one. I loved Jimi Hendrix, I thought he was fantastic and wanted to play like him.

The set I'd put together for my busking featured some of the things that I'd enjoyed playing for years. Kurt Cobain had always been a bit of a hero of mine, so there was some Nirvana in there. But I also played some Bob Dylan and a fair bit by Johnny Cash. One of the most popular things I played was 'Hurt', originally by Nine Inch Nails but then covered by Johnny Cash. It was easier to play that version because it was an acoustic piece. I also played 'The Man In Black' by Johnny Cash. That was a good busking song — and it was kind of appropriate too. I generally wore black. The most popular song in my set was

'Wonderwall' by Oasis. That always worked best, especially outside the pubs when I wandered around later in the evenings.

I played pretty much the same stuff over and over every day. It was what people liked. That's what the tourists wanted to hear. I would usually start with a song like 'About A Girl' by Nirvana just to get the fingers going. That's what I did today, as Bob sat in front of me, watching the crowds walk out of the tube station.

* * *

I'd barely been playing for more than a few minutes when a group of kids stopped. They were obviously from Brazil and were all wearing Brazilian football shirts and speaking what I recognised as Portuguese. One of them, a young girl, bent down and began stroking Bob.

'Ah, *gato bonita*,' she said.

'She is saying you have a beautiful cat,' one of the boys said, helpfully translating her Portuguese.

They were just kids on a trip to London, but they were fascinated. Almost immediately other people were stopping to see what the fuss was about. About half a dozen of the Brazilian kids and other passers-by began fishing around in their pockets and started raining coins into the bag.

'Looks like you may not be such a bad companion after all, Bob. I'll invite you out for the day more often,' I smiled at him.

I'd not planned on bringing him along with

me so I didn't have much to give him. There was a half-empty packet of his favourite cat treats in my rucksack so I gave him one of them every now and again. Like me, he'd have to wait until later to get a decent meal.

As the late afternoon turned into the early evening and the crowds thickened with people heading home from work or out into the West End for the evening, more and more people were slowing down and looking at Bob. There was clearly something about him that fascinated people.

As darkness was beginning to descend, one middle-aged lady stopped for a chat.

'How long have you had him?' she asked, bending down to stroke Bob.

'Oh, only a few weeks,' I said. 'We sort of found each other.'

'Found each other? Sounds interesting.'

At first I was a bit suspicious. I wondered whether she was some kind of animal welfare person and might tell me that I had no right to keep him or something. But she turned out simply to be a real cat lover.

She smiled as I explained the story of how we'd met and how I'd spent a fortnight nursing him back to health.

'I had a ginger tom very much like this one a few years ago,' she said, looking a bit emotional. For a moment I thought she was going to burst into tears. 'You are lucky to have found him. They are just the best companions, they are so quiet and docile. You've found yourself a real friend there,' she said.

'I think you are right,' I smiled.

She placed a fiver into the guitar case before leaving.

He was definitely a lady puller, I realised. I estimated that something like 70 per cent of the people who had stopped so far had been females.

After just over an hour, I had as much as what I'd normally make in a good day, just over twenty-five pounds.

This is brilliant, I thought to myself.

But something inside me was saying that I shouldn't call it quits, that I should carry on for tonight.

The truth was I was still torn about Bob. Despite the gut feeling I had that this cat and I were somehow destined to be together, a large part of me still figured that he'd eventually go off and make his own way. It was only logical. He'd wandered into my life and he was going to wander back out again at some point. This couldn't carry on. So as the passers-by continued to slow down and make a fuss of him, I figured I might as well make the most of it. Make hay while the sun shines and all that.

'If he wants to come out and have fun with me, that's great,' I said to myself. 'And I'm making a bit of cash as well, then that's great too.'

Except that it was more than just a bit of cash by now.

I had been used to making around twenty pounds a day, which was enough to get me through a few days and to cover all the expenses of running my flat. But that night, by the time I finished up at around 8p.m., it was clear that I'd made a lot more than that.

After packing up my guitar, it took me all of five minutes to count out all the coins that had piled up. There were what looked like hundreds of coins of all denominations as well as a few notes scattered amongst them.

When I finally totted it all up, I shook my head quietly. I had made the princely sum of £63.77. To most of the people walking around Covent Garden that might not have seemed like a lot of money. But it was to me.

I transferred all the coins into my rucksack and hauled it on to my shoulders. It was rattling like a giant piggy bank. It also weighed a ton! But I was ecstatic. That was the most I'd ever made in a day's work on the streets, three times what I'd make on a normal day.

I picked up Bob, giving him a stroke on the back of the neck.

'Well done, mate,' I said. 'That was what I call a good evening's work.'

I decided that I didn't need to wander around the pubs. Besides, I knew Bob was hungry — as was I. We needed to head home.

I walked back towards Tottenham Court Road and the bus stop with Bob once more positioned on my shoulder. I wasn't rude to anyone, but I decided not to engage with absolutely everyone who stopped and smiled at us. I couldn't. There were too many of them. I wanted to get home this side of midnight.

'We'll have something nice to eat tonight, Bob,' I said as we settled on to the bus for the trip back up to Tottenham. Again, he pinned his nose up against the window watching the bright lights and the traffic.

I got off the bus near a really nice Indian restaurant on Tottenham High Road. I'd walked past it many times, savouring the lengthy menu, but never had enough spare money to be able to afford anything. I'd always had to make do with something from a cheaper place nearer to the block of flats.

I went in and ordered a chicken tikka masala with lemon rice, a peshwari naan and a sag paneer. The waiters threw me a few, funny looks when they saw Bob on a lead beside me. So I said I'd pop back in twenty minutes and headed off with Bob to a supermarket across the road.

With the money we'd made I treated Bob to a nice pouch of posh cat food, a couple of packs of his favourite nibbles and some 'cat milk'. I also treated myself to a couple of nice tins of lager.

'Let's push the boat out, Bob,' I said to him. 'It's been a day to remember.'

After picking up our dinner, I almost ran home, I was so overwhelmed by the tempting smells coming out from the brown paper carrier bag from the upmarket curry house. When we got inside Bob and I both wolfed down our food as if there was no tomorrow. I hadn't eaten so well in months — well, maybe years. I'm pretty sure he hadn't either.

We then curled up for a couple of hours, me watching television and him snuggled up in his favourite spot under the radiator. We both slept like logs that night.

6

One Man and His Cat

The next morning I was woken by a sudden, loud, crashing sound. It took me a moment to get my bearings, but when I did so I immediately guessed what it was. The metallic, clanging noise had come from the kitchen. That probably meant that once again Bob was trying to open the cupboards where I kept his food and had knocked something over.

I squinted at the clock. It was mid-morning. After the excitement of the previous night I had given myself a lie in, but Bob had obviously decided he couldn't wait any longer. This was his way of saying: 'Get up, I want my breakfast.'

I hauled myself out of bed and stumbled into the kitchen. The small, tin saucepan I used to boil milk was lying on the floor.

As soon as he saw me Bob slid his way purposefully towards his bowl.

'OK, mate, I get the picture,' I said, unlocking the cupboards and reaching for a sachet of his favourite chicken dish. I spooned a couple of portions into the bowl and watched him devour it in seconds. He then gulped down the water in his bowl, licked his face and paws clean and trotted off into the living room, where, looking very satisfied with himself, he took his favourite position under the radiator.

If only all our lives were that simple, I thought to myself.

I'd considered not going to work, but then thought better of it. We may have had a lucky break last night, but that money wouldn't keep us going for long. The electricity and gas bills were due soon. Given the cold weather we'd had in recent months, they weren't going to make for pleasant reading. It had also begun to dawn on me that I had a new responsibility in my life. I had an extra mouth to feed — a rather hungry and manipulative one.

So after wolfing down some breakfast of my own, I started getting my stuff together.

I wasn't sure whether Bob would want to come out busking with me again today. Yesterday might have been a one-off; he might simply have been satisfying his curiosity about where I went when I left home most days. But I put some snacks in the bag for him just in case he did decide to follow me again.

It was early afternoon as I headed off. It was obvious what I was doing; I had my rucksack and guitar lashed across my back. If he didn't want to go out of the flat with me, which was rare, he generally let me know by slinking off behind the sofa. For a moment I thought that was what he was going to do today. When I took the chain off the front door, he headed in that direction. But then as I was about to shut the door behind me he bolted towards me and followed me out into the corridor and towards the staircase.

When we got to the ground floor and out into

the open air he scurried off into the bushes to do his business. Afterwards, rather than heading to me, he trotted off towards the area where the bins were kept.

The bins were becoming more and more of a fascination for him. Goodness knows what he was finding — and eating — in there. I thought that this might be the only reason he'd wanted to come down with me. I wasn't too happy about him rooting around in the rubbish so went to check what was there. You never knew when the local bin men would come. Fortunately, there must have been a collection earlier that morning because there was no stray rubbish around. There were slim pickings, Bob wasn't going to have much joy. Reassured, I decided to head off without him. I knew he'd get back inside the building somehow, especially now that a lot of the neighbours knew him. One or two had started making a real fuss of him whenever they saw him. One lady who lived on the floor below me always gave him a treat.

He would probably be waiting on the landing for me when I got home that evening.

Fair enough, I thought as I set off for Tottenham High Road. Bob had done me a huge favour the previous day. I wasn't going to exploit our relationship by demanding he come along with me every day. He was my companion, not my employee!

The skies were grey and there was a hint of rain in the air. If it was like this in central London it was going to be a waste of time. Busking on a rainy day was never a good idea.

Instead of feeling sympathy for you, people simply rushed by that bit quicker. If it was bucketing down in the centre of town, I told myself, I'd simply turn around and head back home. I would rather spend the day hanging out with Bob. I wanted to use the money we'd made the previous night to get him a decent lead and collar.

I was about two hundred yards or so down the road when I sensed something behind me. I turned round and saw a familiar figure, padding along the pavement.

'Ah, changed our mind have we,' I said, as he approached me.

Bob tilted his head ever so slightly to one side and gave me one of those pitying looks, as if to say: 'well, why else would I be standing here?'

I still had the shoestring lead in my pocket. I put it on and we started walking down the road together.

The streets of Tottenham are very different to those of Covent Garden, but just like the day before people immediately began staring at us. And just like the day before, one or two looked at me disapprovingly. They clearly thought I was off my rocker, leading a ginger tom around on a piece of string.

'If this is going to become a regular thing I really am going to have to get you a proper lead,' I said quietly to Bob, suddenly feeling a bit self-conscious.

But for every person that gave me a dirty look another half dozen smiled and nodded at me. One West Indian lady, weighed down with bags of shopping, gave us a big, sunny grin.

'Don't you two make a pretty picture,' she said.

No one had engaged me in conversation on the streets around my flat in all the months I'd lived here. It was odd, but also amazing. It was as if my Harry Potter invisibility cloak had slipped off my shoulders.

When we got to the crossing point at Tottenham High Road, Bob gave me a look as if to say: 'Come on, you know what to do now' and I plonked him on my shoulders.

Soon we were on the bus, with Bob taking his favourite position with his head pressed against the glass. We were on the road again.

I'd been right about the weather. Soon the rain was hammering down, forming intricate patterns on the window where Bob had once more pressed his face tight against the glass. Outside you could just make out a sea of umbrellas. There were people running, splashing through the streets to avoid the downpour.

Thankfully, the rain had eased off by the time we reached the centre of town. Despite the weather there were even bigger crowds in the centre of town than there had been the previous day.

'We'll give it a go for a couple of hours,' I said to Bob as I plonked him on my shoulders and headed off towards Covent Garden. 'But if it starts to rain again we'll head back, I promise.'

Walking down Neal Street, once again people were stopping us all the time. I was happy to let them fuss over Bob, within reason. In the space of ten minutes, half a dozen people had stopped us and at least half of them had asked to take a picture.

I quickly learned that the key was to keep moving, otherwise you'd be surrounded before you knew it.

It was as we were reaching the end of Neal Street near where I turned towards James Street that something interesting happened.

I suddenly felt Bob's paws readjusting themselves on my shoulder. Before I knew it he was sliding off my shoulder and clambering down my arm. When I let him hop on to the pavement he began walking ahead of me. I extended the lead to its full length and let him go. It was obvious that he recognised where we were and was going to take it from here. He was leading the way.

He marched ahead of me all the way to the pitch where we'd been the previous night. He then stood there, waiting for me to take out my guitar and lay the guitar case down for him.

'There you go, Bob,' I said. He instantly sat down on the soft case as if it was where he belonged. He positioned himself so that he could watch the world walk by — which, this being Covent Garden, it was.

★ ★ ★

There had been a time when I'd had ambitions of making it as a real musician. I'd harboured dreams of becoming the next Kurt Cobain. As naive and completely stupid as it sounds now, it had been part of my grand plan when I'd come back to England from Australia.

That's what I'd told my mother and everyone else when I'd set off.

I'd had my moments and, for a brief time, I felt like I might actually get somewhere.

It was hard for a while, but things changed around 2002, when I'd got off the streets and into some sheltered accommodation in Dalston. One thing had led to another and I'd formed a band with some guys I'd met. We were a four-piece guitar band called Hyper Fury, which told you a lot about my and my band mates' state of mind at the time. The name certainly summed me up. I was an angry young man. I really was hyper-furious — about life in general and about feeling that I'd not had a fair break in particular. My music was an outlet for my anger and angst.

For that reason we weren't very mainstream. Our songs were edgy and dark and our lyrics even more so, which was hardly surprising, I suppose, given that our influences were bands like Nine Inch Nails and Nirvana.

We actually managed to put out two albums, though EPs might be a more accurate description. The first came out in September 2003 with another band, Corrision. It was called *Corrision v Hyper Fury* and featured two pretty heavy tracks, called 'Onslaught' and 'Retaliator'. Again, the titles offer a fairly strong indication to our musical philosophy. We followed that up six months later in March 2004 with a second album called *Profound Destruction Unit*, which featured three songs, 'Sorry', 'Profound' and another version of 'Retaliator'. It sold a few copies but it didn't really set the world on fire. Put it this way: we didn't get booked for Glastonbury.

We did have some fans, though, and managed to get some gigs, mainly in north London and places like Camden, in particular. There was a big Gothy kind of scene going on there and we fitted in well with it. We looked and certainly sounded the part. We did gigs in pubs, we played at squat parties, basically we played wherever we were invited. There was a moment when we might have started to make progress. The biggest gig we did was at The Dublin Castle, a famous music pub in north London, where we played a couple of times. In particular, we played in the Gothic Summer festival there, which was quite a big deal at the time.

Things were going so well for us at one point that I teamed up with a guy called Pete from Corrision and started our own independent label, Corrupt Drive Records.

But it didn't really work or, to be more accurate, I didn't really work.

At the time my best friend Belle and I were in what would be a brief relationship together. We got on great as friends. She is a really caring person and looked after me, but as a relationship it was kind of doomed from the beginning. The problem was that she was on drugs as well and she was co-dependent. It really didn't help me — or her — as we struggled to kick our habits. When one of us was trying to get clean the other one was using and vice versa. That's co-dependency all over.

So it made it really difficult for me to break the cycle.

I was trying to break the cycle, but, looking back on it, if I'm honest I wouldn't say I was trying hard. I think part of it was that I didn't really feel like it was ever going to become a reality. Mentally, at least, the band was something I put on the back-burner. It was too easy to slip back into old habits — quite literally.

By 2005 I'd accepted that the band was a hobby, not a way of making a living. Pete carried on with the record label and still runs it now, I believe. But I was struggling so badly with my habit that I fell by the wayside — again. It became another one of those second chances that I let slip through my fingers. I guess I'll never know what might have been.

I'd never given up on music, however. Even when the band broke up and it was clear that I wasn't going to get anywhere professionally, I would spend hours most days playing on the guitar, improvising songs. It was a great outlet for me. God knows where I'd have been without it. And busking had certainly made a difference to my life in recent years. Without it — and the money it generated — I dread to think what I would have ended up doing to earn cash. That really didn't bear thinking about.

* * *

That evening, as I settled down into the session, the tourists were once more out in force.

It was a repeat of the previous day. The moment

72

I sat down — or, more precisely, the moment Bob sat down — people who would normally have rushed by began to slow down and interact with him.

Again, it was women rather than men who showed the most interest.

Not long after I'd started playing, a rather stony-faced traffic warden walked past. I saw her look down at Bob and watched as her face melted into a warm smile.

'Aah, look at you,' she said, stopping and kneeling down to stroke Bob.

She barely gave me a second glance and didn't drop anything into the guitar case. But that was fine. I was beginning to love the way that Bob seemed to be able to brighten up people's days.

He was a beautiful creature, there was no doubt about that. But it wasn't just that. There was something else about Bob. It was his personality that was attracting the attention. People could sense something about him.

I could sense it myself. There was something special about him. He had an unusual rapport with people, well, people he knew had his best interests at heart, at least.

Every now and again I'd see him bridle a bit when he saw someone he didn't like. As we settled down, a very smart, rich-looking Middle-Eastern guy walked past, arm-in-arm with a really attractive blonde. She could easily have been a model.

'Oh, look. What a gorgeous cat,' she said, suddenly stopping in her tracks and pulling on the guy's arm to slow him down. The guy looked distinctly unimpressed and flicked his hand dismissively, as if to say, 'So what?'

The instant he did so Bob's body language changed. He arched his back ever so slightly and shifted his body position so that he was a few inches closer to me. It was subtle — but to me it was really telling.

I wonder whether this guy reminds Bob of someone from his past? I thought to myself as the couple walked on. *I wonder whether he had seen that look before?*

I'd have given anything to know his story, discover what had led him to the hallway of my block of flats that evening. But that was something I never was going to know. It would always be guesswork.

As I settled into my set I was much more relaxed than twenty-four hours earlier. I think having Bob there the previous day had thrown me a bit, psychologically. I'd been used to having to engage and draw in the crowds myself. It had been hard work. Eking out every penny was tough. With Bob it was different. The way he'd sucked in the audience for me had been a bit odd at first. I'd also felt very responsible for him with so many people around. Covent Garden — like the rest of London — has its share of weirdos. I was terrified that someone would just grab him and run off with him.

But that day felt different, however. That day I felt like we were safe, like we kind of belonged here.

As I began singing and the coins started tinkling into the case at the same rate as the previous day, I thought to myself: *I'm enjoying this*.

It had been a long time since I'd said that.

★ ★ ★

By the time we headed home three hours later my rucksack was once more jangling with the weight of coins. We'd collected well over sixty pounds again.

This time I wasn't going to spend it on an expensive curry. I had more practical uses for the money. The following day the weather was even worse, with the forecast of really heavy rain that night.

So I decided to spend some time on Bob rather than busking. If he was going to hang out with me on a regular basis then I needed to have better equipment for him. I couldn't walk around with him attached to a leash made out of a shoelace. Apart from anything else, it was uncomfortable — not to mention dangerous.

Bob and I hopped on a bus and headed off in the direction of Archway. I knew the north London branch of the Cats Protection charity was there.

Bob seemed to sense immediately that this wasn't the same route we'd taken the previous couple of days. Every now and again he would turn and look at me as if to say: 'So, where are you taking me today?' He wasn't anxious, just curious.

The Cats Protection shop was a smart, modern place with all sorts of equipment, toys

75

and books about cats. There were loads of free pamphlets and brochures on every aspect of caring for a cat — from microchipping to toxoplasmosis, diet tips to neutering advice. I picked up a few for future reading.

There were only a couple of people working there and the place was quiet. So they couldn't resist coming over for a chat as I took a look around with Bob sitting on my shoulder.

'He's a good-looking boy isn't he?' one lady said, stroking Bob. He could tell he was in safe hands because he was leaning his body into her as she smoothed his coat and cooed over him.

We then fell into a conversation about how Bob and I had met. I then explained what had happened the previous two days. Both women smiled and nodded.

'A lot of cats like to go out for a walk with their owners,' one told me. 'They like to go for a walk in the park or for a short stroll down the street. But I have to say Bob's a bit unusual isn't he?'

'He is,' her friend said. 'I think you've got yourself a bit of a jewel there. He's obviously decided to attach himself to you.'

It was nice to hear them confirming what, deep down, I knew already. Every now and again, I had a little pang of doubt about whether I should try harder to put him back on the streets, whether I was doing the right thing in keeping him in the flat with me. Their words were a real boost for me.

What I didn't know, however, was how best to manage Bob if he was going to be my constant companion on the streets of London. It wasn't the safest of environments, to put it mildly. Apart from the obvious traffic, there were all sorts of potential threats and dangers out there.

'The best thing you can do is to get a harness like this,' one of the ladies said, unhooking a nice-looking blue, woven nylon harness, collar and matching lead.

She explained the pros and cons of it.

'It's not a great idea just to fix a leash to a cat collar. The worst collars can harm your cat's neck and even choke the cat. And the problem with the better quality collars is that they are made from elastic or are what they call 'breakaway' collars so that the cat can escape if the collar gets caught on something. There's a good chance that at some point you'll have an empty leash dangling in your hand,' the lady explained. 'I think you would be much better off with a cat harness and a leash, especially given you are out all the time,' she said.

'Isn't it going to feel funny for him?' I asked. 'It's not going to feel natural.'

'You'll need to ease him into it,' she agreed. 'It might take you a week or so. Start him off wearing it for a few minutes a day before you are ready to go outside together. Then build it up from there.' She could see me mulling it over. 'Why not try it on him?'

'Why not?' I said.

Bob was sitting comfortably and didn't offer too much resistance, although I could tell that he was uncertain about what was happening.

'Just leave it on him and let him get used to

the sensation of having it on his body,' the lady said.

The harness, lead and collar cost about thirteen pounds. It was one of the most expensive they had, but I figured he was worth it.

If I'd been a businessman, chief executive of James & Bob Inc, I'd have been thinking you've got to look after your employees, you've got to invest in your human resources — except in this case it was my feline resources.

★ ★ ★

It only took me a couple of days to introduce Bob to the harness. I began just by letting him wear it around the house, sometimes with the lead attached. At first he was a bit confused at having this extra-long, leather tail trailing behind him. But he soon got used to it. Every time he wore it I made sure to praise him for doing so. I knew the worst thing I could do was to shout at him, not that I ever did that anyway.

After a couple of days we progressed to going on short walks with it on. When we were out busking, I stuck to the old collar most of the time, but then every now and again I'd slip the harness on for a short section of the walk to work. Slowly but surely it became second nature to him to have the harness on.

Bob was still coming with me every day.

We didn't stay out too long. I didn't want to inflict that on him. Even though I already had a feeling he would follow me to the ends of the earth, and even though he was always sitting on

78

my shoulders and didn't have to walk, I wasn't going to do that to him.

It was during the third week of us busking together that he first decided he didn't want to join me. Ordinarily, the minute he saw me putting on my coat and packing my rucksack, he'd be up and moving towards me, ready for me to put his lead on. But then, one day, as I went through the normal routine, he just shuffled off behind the sofa for a bit then went and laid down underneath the radiator. It was as if to say 'I'm having a day off.'

I could tell he was tired.

'Don't fancy it today, Bob?' I said, stroking him.

He looked at me in that knowing way of his.

'No problem,' I said, heading to the kitchen to put some snacks in a bowl to keep him going for the rest of the day until I got home that evening.

I'd read a report once that said leaving the TV on made pets feel less lonely when their owners are out. I didn't know whether that was true, but I switched the TV set on in any case. He immediately shuffled towards his favourite spot and started staring at it.

★ ★ ★

Going out that day really brought home to me the difference Bob had made to my life. With him on my shoulder or walking on the lead in front of me, I turned heads everywhere. On my own I was invisible again. By now we were well known enough to the locals for a few people to express concern.

'Where's the cat today?' one local stall-owner said as he passed me by that evening.

'He's having a day off,' I said.

'Oh, good. I was worried something had happened to the little fella,' he smiled, giving me the thumbs-up.

A couple of other people stopped and asked the same question. As soon as I'd told them Bob was fine they moved on. No one was quite as interested in stopping for a talk as they did when Bob was around. I may not have liked it, but I accepted it. That's the way it was.

On the pavement at James Street, the sound of coins landing in the bag had become music to my ears; I couldn't deny that. But without Bob I couldn't help noticing that the music slowed down significantly. As I played I was conscious that I wasn't making anywhere near as much money. It took me a few more hours to earn about half the cash I had made on a good day with Bob. It was back to the old days before Bob, but that was OK.

It was as I walked back that evening that something began to sink in. It wasn't all about making money. I wasn't going to starve. And my life was much richer for having Bob in it.

It was such a pleasure to have such great company, such a great companion. But somehow it felt like I'd been given a chance to get back on track.

It's not easy when you are working on the streets. People don't want to give you a chance. Before I had Bob, if I would try to approach people in the pubs with my guitar strap on, people would go 'no, sorry' before I'd even had a chance to say hello.

I could have been asking someone for the time. But they'd say to me: 'no change, sorry' before I opened my mouth. That happened all the time. They wouldn't even give me the opportunity.

People don't want to listen. All they see is someone they think is trying to get a free ride. They don't understand I'm working, I'm not begging. I was actually trying to make a living. Just because I wasn't wearing a suit and a tie and carrying a briefcase or a computer, just because I didn't have a payslip and a P45, it didn't mean that I was freeloading.

Having Bob there gave me a chance to interact with people.

They would ask about Bob and I would get a chance to explain my situation at the same time. They would ask where he came from and I'd then be able to explain how we got together and how we were making money to pay our rent, food, electricity and gas bills. People would give me more of a fair hearing.

Psychologically, people also began to see me in a different light.

Cats are notoriously picky about who they like. And if a cat doesn't like its owner it will go and find another one. Cats do that all the time. They go and live with somebody else. Seeing me with my cat softened me in their eyes. It humanised me. Especially after I'd been so dehumanised. In some ways it was giving me back my identity. I had been a non-person; I was becoming a person again.

7

The Two Musketeers

Bob wasn't just changing people's attitude to me: he was changing my attitude to others as well.

I'd never really had any responsibilities towards others in my life. I'd had the odd job here and there when I was younger in Australia and I'd also been in a band, which required a bit of teamwork. But the truth was that, since I left home as a teenager, my main responsibility had always been to myself. I'd always had to look after number one, simply because there wasn't anyone else to do it. As a result, my life had become a very selfish one. It was all about my day-today survival.

Bob's arrival in my life had dramatically changed all that. I'd suddenly taken on an extra responsibility. Another being's health and happiness was down to me.

It had come as a bit of a shock, but I had begun to adapt to it. In fact, I enjoyed it. I knew it may sound silly to a lot of people, but for the first time I had an idea what it must be like looking after a child. Bob was my baby and making sure he was warm, well fed and safe was really rewarding. It was scary too.

I worried about him constantly, in particular, when I was out on the streets. In Covent Garden and elsewhere I was always in protective mode, my instincts were always telling me that I had to watch out for him at every turn. With good cause.

I hadn't been lulled into a false sense of security by the way people treated me with Bob. The streets of London weren't all filled with kind-hearted tourists and cat lovers. Not everyone was going to react the same way when they saw a long-haired busker and his cat singing for their suppers on street corners. It happened less now that I had Bob, but I still got a volley of abuse every now and again, usually from drunken young blokes who felt the fact they were picking up a pay packet at the end of the week made them somehow superior to me.

'Get off your arse and do a proper day's work you long-haired layabout,' they would say, albeit almost always in more colourful language than that.

I let their insults wash over me. I was used to them. It was a different matter when people turned their aggression on Bob. That's when my protective instincts really took over.

Some people saw me and Bob as easy targets. Almost every day, we'd be approached by idiots of some kind. They would shout stupid comments or stand there laughing at us. Occasionally, they would threaten to turn violent.

One Friday evening, quite soon after Bob and I had first come to Covent Garden together, I was playing at James Street when a bunch of young, very rowdy, black lads came past. They had real attitude, and were obviously on the lookout for trouble. A couple of them spotted Bob sitting on the pavement next to me and started making 'woof' and 'meow' noises, much to the amusement of their mates.

I could have coped with that. It was just stupid, puerile stuff. But then, for no reason whatsoever, one of them kicked the guitar case with Bob sitting in it. It wasn't a playful tap with his toes, it had real venom in it, and sent the case — and Bob — sliding a foot or so along the pavement.

Bob was really distressed. He made a loud noise, almost like a scream, and jumped out of the case. Thankfully his lead was attached to the case otherwise he would almost certainly have run off into the crowds. I might never have seen him again. Instead, restrained by the lead, he had no option but to hide behind my rucksack, which was standing nearby.

I got up immediately and confronted the guy.

'What the f*** did you do that for?' I said, standing toe-to-toe with him. I'm quite tall and towered over him, but it didn't seem to faze him.

'I just wanted to see if the cat was real,' he said, laughing as if he'd cracked a brilliant joke.

I didn't see the funny side of it.

'That's really clever, you f****** idiot,' I said.

That was the signal for it all to kick off. They all began circling me and one of them began shoving into me with his chest and shoulders, but I stood my ground and shoved him back. For a split second or two there was a stand-off, but then I pointed to a CCTV camera that I knew was positioned on the corner near us.

'Go on then, do what you want. But just remember: you're on camera; see how far you get afterwards.'

The look on their faces was a picture I'd love to have captured — on CCTV or anywhere. They were obviously street smart enough to know you couldn't get away with violence on camera. One of them gave me a look as if to say: 'I will get you for that.'

Of course, they couldn't back down without raining down another wave of insults. But they were soon moving on, waving their arms and making every offensive gesture known to man. Sticks and stones and all that. I wasn't worried. In fact, I felt good about seeing them off. But I didn't hang around much longer that evening. I knew their type. They didn't take kindly to being 'dissed'.

The incident proved a couple of things to me. First, it was always a good idea to be near a CCTV camera. It had been another busker who had first given me the advice to always try and pitch yourself near one. 'You'll be safer there,' he said. Of course, I was too much of a know-all back then. Wasn't it going to give the authorities evidence if I was busking illegally? I'd ignored the advice for a while. Slowly but surely, however, I'd seen the wisdom of his words and incidents like this underlined them.

That was the positive. The negative was that I'd been reminded of something I'd also known. I really was on my own when trouble flared like this. There wasn't a policeman in sight. There wasn't a whiff of a Covent Guardian or even any assistance from the staff in the tube station. Despite the fact that quite a lot of people were milling around when the gang confronted me, none of the passers-by offered to intervene. In fact, people did their best to melt into the background and shuffle off. Nobody was going to come to my aid. In that respect, nothing had changed. Except, of course, I now had Bob.

As we headed back up to Tottenham that evening he cozied up to me on the bus. 'It's you and me against the world,' I said to him. 'We're the two Musketeers.'

He nuzzled up to me and purred lightly, as if in agreement.

The hard reality was that London was full of people who we had to treat with caution. Ever since I'd started bringing Bob with me I'd been wary of dogs, for instance. There were a lot of them, obviously, and it was no surprise that many of them took an instant interest in Bob. To be fair, in the vast majority of cases, people would notice if their dog was getting too close and give them a gentle tug on the lead. But others came too close for my comfort.

Fortunately Bob didn't seem to be bothered about them at all. He just ignored them. If they came up to him he would just stare them out. Again, it underlined my suspicion that he'd begun his life on the streets, he'd learned to handle himself there. Just how well he could handle himself I found out a week or so after the incident with the gang.

We were sitting in Neal Street in the late

afternoon when a guy with a Staffordshire Bull Terrier loomed into view. Arseholes always have Staffs, it's a fact of London life, and this guy really looked like an arsehole. He was shaven-headed, swigging extra-strength lager and wearing a tatty tracksuit. From the way he was slaloming around the street, he was off his head already, even though it was barely 4p.m.

They slowed down when they got to us purely because the Staff was straining at the leash as it tried to move in the direction of me and Bob.

As it happened, the dog wasn't threatening, he was just checking Bob out. Well, not even that, he was checking out the biscuits Bob had in front of him. He wasn't eating them at the time so the Staffie started inching his way towards the bowl, sniffing excitedly at the prospect of a free titbit or two.

I couldn't believe what happened next.

I'd seen Bob around dogs a fair bit by now. His normal policy was not to give them the time of day. On this occasion, however, he must have felt some action was necessary.

He'd been snoozing peacefully at my side. But as the Staffie leaned in towards the biscuits, he calmly looked up, picked himself up and then just bopped the dog on the nose with his paw. It was so lightning fast it was a punch to do Muhammad Ali proud.

The dog couldn't believe it. He just jumped back in shock and then carried on backtracking.

I was almost as shocked as the dog, I think. I just laughed out loud.

The owner looked at me and then looked

down at his dog. I think he was so drunk he couldn't fully comprehend what had just happened, especially as it had occurred in the blink of an eye. He gave the dog a whack around the head then tugged on its lead to move on. I think he was embarrassed that his fearsome-looking beast had been made to look stupid by a cat.

Bob watched quietly as the dog, his head hung in shame, walked away. Within a few seconds he'd reverted back to his previous position, snoozing at my feet. It was as if it was a minor annoyance for him, like swatting a pesky fly. But for me it was a really revealing moment. It told me so much more about my companion and the life he had led before our fateful meeting at the bottom of the stairs. He wasn't afraid to defend himself. In fact, he knew how to look after himself rather well. He must have learned to do that somewhere, maybe in an environment where there were lots of dogs — and aggressive ones at that.

Once more I found myself fascinated by the same old questions. Where had he grown up? What adventures had he had before he had joined up with me and become the second Musketeer?

★ ★ ★

Living with Bob was fun. As our little run-in with the Staffie proved, there was never a dull moment. He was a real personality, of that there was no doubt. He had all sorts of quirks to his character, and I was discovering more and more of them every day.

By now there was little doubt in my mind that he must have grown up on the streets. It wasn't just his street-fighter skills, he wasn't really domesticated in any way, he was a bit rough around the edges. Even now, after he'd been living with me for the best part of a month, he still didn't like using the litter trays I'd bought for him. He really hated those things and would scamper away whenever I put one down anywhere near him. Instead he would hold on until he saw me going out of the door, and then do his business downstairs in the gardens of the flats.

I didn't want it to carry on like this. For a start, it wasn't much fun walking down — and up — five flights of stairs to take the cat out whenever he wanted to go to the toilet. So I decided to try and give Bob no option but to use the litter trays. One day during that third week I said to myself that I would go twenty-four hours without letting him out, so that he would have no alternative but to use the litter tray. But he won that contest hands down. He bottled everything up and waited — and waited and waited until I had to go out. Then he squeezed past me as I went out the door and bolted down the stairwell to get outside. Game, set and match to Bob. I realised it was a fight I was unlikely to win.

He also had a wild side to his personality. He was calmer than when he'd first arrived, thanks largely to the fact that he'd been neutered. But he could still be a complete maniac around the flat and would frequently tear around the place, playing with anything that he could lay his paws on. One day I watched him amuse himself for the best part of an hour with a bottle top, flipping it around the floor of the living room with his paws. Another time he found a bumblebee. It was obviously injured — it had one wing damaged — so it was struggling around on the coffee table in the living room. The bee was rolling around and every now and again it would fall off the table on to the carpet. Every time this happened, Bob would very gently pick it up with his teeth and put it back on the table. It was really impressive the way he could delicately pick the bee up by the wing and place it safely on the flat surface. He'd then watch it while it struggled around again. It was a really comical sight. He didn't want to eat it. He just wanted to play with it.

The street instinct was still apparent when it came to food as well. When I took him downstairs to do his toilet now, he made a beeline for the area at the back of the flats where the dustbins were kept. The large 'wheelie bins' were often left open and occasionally there were discarded black, plastic refuse sacks, that had been ripped open by urban foxes or stray dogs. Bob would always go and investigate them to see if there were any leftovers. On one occasion I'd caught him dragging a chicken drumstick that had somehow been overlooked by the other scavengers. Old habits die hard, I figured.

It was true, of course. Despite the fact I was

feeding him on a regular basis, he still treated every meal as if it was going to be his last. At home in the flat, the moment I scooped some cat food into his bowl he would stick his face in it and start guzzling as if there was no tomorrow.

'Slow down and enjoy your food, Bob,' I'd tell him, but to no avail. Again, I figured he'd spent so long having to make the most of every eating opportunity that he hadn't adapted to living in a place where he was guaranteed a square meal twice a day. I knew how that felt. I'd spent large chunks of my life living the same way. I couldn't really blame him.

Bob and I had so much in common. Maybe that was why the bond had formed so fast — and was growing so deep.

★ ★ ★

The most irritating thing — literally — about him, however, was the fact that his fur had begun coating every corner of the flat.

It was perfectly natural, of course. Spring was here and he was getting rid of his winter coat. But he was starting to lose a hell of a lot of fur. To help the moulting process he was rubbing himself on anything and everything he could find in the flat. As a result he was covering it in a thick film of fur. It was a real pain.

It was a good sign that his coat — and the rest of his body — was returning to good health. He was still a bit scrawny, but there was no sign of his ribs as there had been when I'd first met him. His coat was naturally thin because of the environment he'd probably grown up in — the street. The medication had helped with his bald patches and the antibiotics had definitely done the trick in healing his old wound. That had almost disappeared now, in fact, if you didn't know it was there you would never have noticed it.

All in all he looked in a lot better nick than he had done a month or so earlier.

I didn't bathe him. Cats wash themselves, and he was a typical cat in that respect, regularly licking and washing himself. In fact, Bob was one of the most meticulous cats I'd ever seen. I'd watch him go through the ritual, methodically licking his paws. It fascinated me, especially the fact that it was linked so strongly to his ancient ancestors.

Bob's distant relatives originated from hot climates and didn't sweat, so licking themselves was their way of releasing saliva and cooling themselves down. It was also their version of the invisibility cloak.

Smell is bad for cats from a hunting point of view. Cats are stealth hunters and ambush their prey, so they have to be as unobtrusive as possible. Cat saliva contains a natural deodorant which is why they lick themselves a lot. It's been proven by zoologists that cats that lick the smell off themselves survive longer and have more successful offspring. It's also their way of hiding themselves from predators like large snakes, lizards and other larger carnivorous mammals.

Of course, the most important reason that Bob and his ancestors had always licked themselves was to establish and maintain good health. Cats effectively self-medicate. Licking cuts down the number of parasites, such as lice, mites and ticks that can potentially damage the cat. It also stops infection in any open wounds, as cats' saliva also contains an antiseptic agent. As I watched him one day, it occurred to me that this might be why Bob was licking himself so regularly. He knew his body had been in a bad way. This was his way of helping the healing process.

The other funny habit he'd developed was watching television. I first noticed that he watched things on screens one day when I was playing around on a computer in the local library. I often popped in there on the way to Covent Garden or when I wasn't busking. I'd taken Bob along for a walk. He had decided to sit on my lap and was staring at the screen with me. I noticed that as I was moving the mouse around he was trying to swat the cursor with his paw. So back at the flat, as an experiment one day, I'd just put the TV on and left the room to go and do something in the bedroom. I came back to find Bob ensconced on the sofa, watching.

I'd heard about cats watching TV from a friend whose cat loved *Star Trek: The Next Generation*. Whenever it heard that familiar music — Dah-Dah Dah Dah Dah-Dah Dah Dah — he'd come running into the room and jump on the sofa. I saw it happen a few times and it was hilarious. No joke.

Pretty soon, Bob had become a bit of a telly addict as well. If something caught his eye, then he suddenly was glued to the screen. I found it really funny watching him watching Channel Four racing. He really liked the horses. It wasn't something I watched but I got a real kick from watching him sitting there fascinated by it.

8

Making It Official

One Thursday morning, a few weeks after we had started our busking partnership in Covent Garden, I got up earlier than usual, made us both some breakfast and headed out of the door with Bob. Rather than heading for central London as usual, we got off the bus near Islington Green.

I'd made a decision. With him accompanying me almost every day on the streets now, I needed to do the responsible thing and get Bob microchipped.

Microchipping cats and dogs used to be a complicated business but now it's simple. All it requires is a simple surgical procedure in which a vet injects a tiny chip into the cat's neck. The chip contains a serial number, which is then logged against their owner's details. That way if a stray cat is found people can scan the chip and find out where it belongs.

Given the life Bob and I led, I figured it was a good idea to get it done. If, God forbid, we ever got separated, we'd be able to find each other. If worse came to worst and something happened to me, at least the records would show that Bob wasn't a completely feral street cat; he had once been in a loving home.

When I'd first begun researching the micro-chipping process in the library I had quickly come to the conclusion that I couldn't afford it. Most vets were charging an extortionate sixty to eighty pounds to insert a chip. I just didn't have that kind of money and, even if I did, I wouldn't have paid that much on principle.

But then one day I got talking to the cat lady across the street.

'You should go along to the Blue Cross van in Islington Green on a Thursday,' she said. 'They just charge for the cost of the chip. But make sure you get there early. There's always a big queue.'

So I'd set off today nice and early to get to that morning's clinic, which I knew ran from 10a.m. to noon.

As the cat lady had predicted, we discovered a lengthy queue when we got to Islington Green. A long line stretched down towards the big Waterstone's bookshop. Luckily it was a bright, clear morning so it wasn't a problem hanging around.

There was the usual collection you find in a situation like that; people with their cats in posh carriers, dogs trying to sniff each other and being a general nuisance. But it was quite sociable and it was certainly a smarter, more caring crowd than at the RSPCA where I'd first taken Bob to be checked out.

What was funny was that Bob was the only cat that wasn't in a carrier, so he attracted a lot of attention — as usual. There were a couple of elderly ladies who were absolutely smitten and kept fussing over him.

After about an hour and a half queuing, Bob

and I reached the front of the line where we were greeted by a young veterinary nurse with short bobbed hair.

'How much will it cost to get him microchipped?' I asked her.

'It's fifteen pounds,' she replied.

It was pretty obvious from my appearance that I wasn't exactly rolling in money. So she quickly added, 'But you don't have to pay it all up front. You can pay it off over a few weeks. Say two pounds a week, how's that?'

'Cool,' I said, pleasantly surprised. 'I can do that.'

She gave Bob a quick check, presumably to make sure he was in decent-enough health, which he was. He was looking a lot healthier these days, especially now that he had fully shed his winter coat. He was lean and really athletic.

She led us into the surgery where the vet was waiting. He was a young guy, in his late twenties, probably.

'Morning,' he said to me before turning to chat to the nurse. They had a quiet confab in the corner and then started preparing for the chipping procedure. I watched as they got the stuff together. The nurse got out some paperwork while the vet produced the syringe and needle to inject the chip. The size of it slightly took my breath away. It was a big old needle. But then I realised it had to be if it was going to insert the chip, which was the size of a large grain of rice. It had to be large enough to get into the animal's skin.

Bob didn't like the look of it at all, and I

couldn't really blame him. So the nurse and I got hold of him and tried to turn him away from the vet so that he couldn't see what he was doing.

Bob wasn't stupid, however, and knew something was up. He got quite agitated and tried to wriggle his way out of my grip. 'You'll be OK, mate,' I said, stroking his tummy and hind legs, while the vet closed in.

When the needle penetrated, Bob let out a loud squeal. It cut through me like a knife and for a moment I thought I was going to start blubbing when he began shaking in pain.

But the shaking soon dissipated and he calmed down. I gave him a little treat from my rucksack then carefully scooped him up and headed back to the reception area.

'Well done, mate,' I said.

The nurse asked me to go through a couple of complicated-looking forms. Fortunately the information she wanted was pretty straightforward.

'OK, we need to fill in your details so that they are on the database,' she said. 'We will need your name, address, age, phone number all that kind of stuff,' she smiled.

It was only as I watched the nurse filling in the form that it struck me. Did this mean that I was officially Bob's owner?

'So, legally speaking, does that mean I am now registered as his owner?' I asked the girl.

She just looked up from the paperwork and smiled. 'Yes, is that OK?' she said.

'Yeah, that's great,' I said slightly taken aback. 'Really great.'

By now Bob was settling down a little. I gave him a stroke on the front of the head. He was obviously still feeling the injection so I didn't go near his neck, he'd have scratched my arm off.

'Did you hear that, Bob?' I said. 'Looks like we're officially a family.'

I'm sure I drew even more looks than usual as we walked through Islington afterwards. I must have been wearing a smile as wide as the Thames.

★ ★ ★

Having Bob with me had already made a difference to the way I was living my life. He'd made me clean up my act in more ways than one.

As well as giving me more routine and a sense of responsibility, he had also made me take a good look at myself. I didn't like what I saw.

I wasn't proud of the fact I was a recovering addict and I certainly wasn't proud of the fact that I had to visit a clinic once a fortnight and collect medication from a pharmacy every day. So I made it a rule that, unless it was absolutely necessary, I wouldn't take him with me on those trips. I know it may sound crazy, but I didn't want him seeing that side of my past. That was something else he'd helped me with; I really did see it as my past. I saw my future as being clean, living a normal life. I just had to complete the long journey that led to that point.

There were still plenty of reminders of that past and of how far I had still to travel. A few days after I'd had him microchipped, I was rummaging around looking for the new Oyster card that had come through the post when I started emptying the contents of a cupboard in my bedroom.

There, at the back of the cupboard, under a pile of old newspapers and clothes, was a plastic Tupperware box. I recognised it immediately, although I hadn't seen it for a while. It contained all the paraphernalia I had collected when I was doing heroin. There were syringes, needles, everything I had needed to feed my habit. It was like seeing a ghost. It brought back a lot of bad memories. I saw images of myself that I really had hoped to banish from my mind forever.

I decided immediately that I didn't want that box in the house any more. I didn't want it there to remind and maybe even tempt me. And I definitely didn't want it around Bob, even though it was hidden away from view.

Bob was sitting next to the radiator as usual but got up when he saw me putting my coat on and getting ready to go downstairs. He followed me all the way down to the bin area and watched me as I threw the box into a recycling container for hazardous waste.

'There,' I said, turning to Bob who was now fixing me with one of his inquisitive stares. 'Just doing something I should have done a long time ago.'

9

The Escape Artist

Life on the streets is never straightforward. You've always got to expect the unexpected. I learned that early on. Social workers always use the word 'chaotic' when they talk about people like me. They call our lives chaotic, because they don't conform to their idea of normality, but it is normality to us. So I wasn't surprised when, as that first summer with Bob drew to a close and autumn began, life around Covent Garden started to get more complicated. I knew it couldn't stay the same. Nothing ever did in my life.

Bob was still proving a real crowd-pleaser, especially with tourists. Wherever they came from, they would stop and talk to him. By now I think I'd heard every language under the sun — from Afrikaans to Welsh — and learned the word for cat in all of them. I knew the Czech name, *kocka* and Russian, *koshka*; I knew the Turkish, *kedi* and my favourite, the Chinese, *mao*. I was really surprised when I discovered their great leader had been a cat!

But no matter what weird or wonderful tongue was being spoken, the message was almost always the same. Everyone loved Bob.

We also had a group of 'regulars', people who worked in the area and passed by on their way home in the evening. A few of them would always stop to say hello. One or two had even started giving Bob little presents.

It was the other 'locals' who were causing the problems.

To begin with I'd been getting a bit of hassle over at James Street from the Covent Guardians. I'd been continuing to play next to the tube station. On a couple of occasions a Guardian had come over and spoken to me. He'd laid down the law, explaining that the area was for painted statues. The fact that there didn't seem to be any around at that moment didn't bother him. 'You know the rules,' he kept telling me. I did. But I also knew rules were there to be bent a little when they could be. Again, that was life on the streets. If we were the kind of people who stuck to the rules, we wouldn't have been there.

So each time the Guardian moved me on, I'd head off elsewhere for a few hours then quietly slip back into James Street. It was a risk worth taking as far as I was concerned. I'd never heard of them calling in the police to deal with someone performing in the wrong place.

The people who were bothering me much more were the staff at the tube station who also now seemed to object to me busking outside their workplace. There were a couple of ticket inspectors in particular who had begun giving me a hard time. It had begun as dirty looks and the odd casual comment when I set myself up against the wall of the tube station. But then one really unpleasant inspector, a big, sweaty guy in a blue uniform, had come over to me one day and been quite threatening.

By now I had come to realise that Bob was a great reader of people. He could spot someone who wasn't quite right from a distance. He had spotted this guy the minute he started walking in our direction and had started squeezing himself closer to me as he approached.

'All right, mate?' I said.

'Not really. No. You had better piss off — or else,' he said.

'Or else what?' I said, standing my ground.

'You'll see,' he said obviously trying to intimidate me. 'I'm warning you.'

I knew he had no power outside the tube station and was just trying to spook me. But afterwards I'd made the decision that it might be smart to stay away for a while.

★   ★   ★

So at first I'd moved to the top of Neal Street, near the junction with Long Acre, still no more than a healthy stone's throw from the tube station but far enough to be out of sight of the staff. The volume of people passing there wasn't as great — or always as well-meaning — as the people around Covent Garden. Most times I worked there I'd get some idiot kicking my bag or trying to scare Bob. I could tell he wasn't comfortable there: he'd curl up in a defensive ball and narrow his eyes to a thin slit whenever I set up there. It was his way of saying: 'I don't like it here.'

So after a few days, rather than heading

towards Covent Garden as usual, Bob and I climbed off the bus and walked through Soho in the direction of Piccadilly Circus instead.

Of course, we hadn't left central London — and the borough of Westminster — so there were still rules and regulations. Piccadilly worked in a similar way to Covent Garden; there were certain areas that were designated for buskers. This time I decided to stick to the rules. I knew that the area to the east of Piccadilly Circus on the road leading to Leicester Square was a good spot, specifically for buskers. So I headed there.

Arriving there with Bob, I picked a spot only a few yards away from one of the main entrances to the Piccadilly Circus tube station, outside the Ripley's Believe It Or Not exhibition.

It was a really busy late afternoon and evening with hundreds of tourists on the street, heading to the West End's cinemas and theatres. We were soon doing all right, despite the fact that people move so fast around that area, running down the tube entrance. As usual, they slowed down and sometimes stopped when they saw Bob.

I could tell Bob was a little nervous because he curled himself up even tighter than usual around the bridge of my guitar. It was probably the number of people and the fact that he was in unfamiliar surroundings. He was definitely more comfortable when he was in a place that he recognised.

As usual, people from all over the world were milling around, taking in the sights of central London. There were a lot of Japanese tourists in particular, a lot of whom were fascinated by Bob.

I'd soon learned another new word for cat: *neko*. Everything was fine until around six in the evening, when the crowds really thickened with the beginning of the rush hour. It was at that point that a promotions guy from Ripley's came out on to the street. He was wearing a big, inflatable outfit that made him look three times his normal size and was making big arm gestures encouraging people to visit Ripley's. I had no idea how it related to the exhibits inside the building. Maybe they had something on the world's fattest man? Or the world's most ridiculous job?

But I could tell immediately that Bob didn't like the look of him. I sensed him drawing in even closer to me when he first appeared. He was really unsure of the bloke and was staring at him with a look of slight trepidation. I knew exactly where he was coming from; he did look a bit freaky.

To my relief, after a while Bob settled down and seemed to forget about the man. For a while we just ignored him as he carried on trying to persuade people to step into Ripley's. He was having some success, so he stayed away from us. I was singing a Johnny Cash song, 'Ring of Fire', when, for no particular reason, the promotions guy suddenly approached us, pointing at Bob as if he wanted to come and stroke him. I didn't spot him until he was almost upon us, leaning down in his weird inflatable suit. And by then it was too late.

Bob's reaction was instantaneous. He just sprung up and bolted, running into the crowds with his new lead trailing behind him. Before I could even react, he'd disappeared, heading towards the entrance to the tube station.

Oh shit, I said to myself, my heart pumping. *He's gone. I've lost him.*

My instincts took over at once. I jumped up straight away and ran after him. I just left the guitar. I was much more worried about Bob than an instrument. I could find one of those anywhere.

I immediately found myself in a sea of people. There were weary-looking office workers heading down the tube at the end of a day's work, early evening revellers arriving for a night 'up West' and, as always, loads and loads of tourists, some with rucksacks, others clutching streetmaps, all looking a little overwhelmed at finding themselves at the beating heart of London. I had to bob and weave my way through them to even get to the entrance to the tube station. Inevitably, I bumped into a couple of people, almost knocking over one lady.

It was impossible to see anything through the constant wall of people that was moving towards me, but as I finally got to the bottom of the steps inside the concourse, things began to thin out a little bit. It was still heaving with people, but at least I could now stop and take a look around. I got down on my haunches and looked around at floor level. One or two people gave me strange looks but that didn't concern me.

'Bob, Bob, where are you, mate?' I shouted at one point, immediately realising how futile that was with all the noise in there.

I had to make a guess and head in one direction. Should I go towards the barriers that led to the escalators and down to the trains or move towards the various other exits? Which way would Bob go? My hunch was that he wouldn't go down the tube. We'd never been down there together and I had a feeling the moving escalators would frighten him.

So I moved towards the exits for the other side of Piccadilly Circus.

After a moment or two, I got a glimpse of something, just the faintest flash of ginger on one of the staircases. I then saw a lead trailing after it.

'Bob, Bob,' I shouted again, squeezing myself through the crowds once more as I headed in that direction.

I was now within thirty feet of him but I might as well have been a mile away, the crowds were so thick. There were streams of people coming down the staircase.

'Stop him, step on his lead,' I shouted out, catching another glimpse of ginger in the evening light above me.

But no one was taking any notice. No was paying any attention.

Within moments the lead had disappeared and there was no sign of Bob. He must have reached the exit, which led to the bottom of Regent Street and run off from there.

By now a million thoughts were flashing through my head, none of them good ones. What if he had run out into the road at Piccadilly Circus? What if someone had seen him and picked him up? As I barged my way up the stairs and reached street level again I was in a real state.

Truth be told, I could have burst into tears, I was so convinced that I'd never see him again.

I knew it wasn't my fault, but I felt awful. Why the hell hadn't I fixed his lead to my rucksack or on to my belt so that he couldn't run any further than the length of his lead? Why hadn't I spotted his panic when the Ripley's guy had first appeared and moved somewhere else? I felt sick.

Again I had to make a choice. Which way would he have headed on hitting the streets? He could have turned left towards Piccadilly or even headed into the giant Tower Records store there. Again I trusted my instincts and guessed that he would have basically headed straight on — down the wider pavements of Regent Street.

Still in a complete panic, I began making my way down the street in the hope that someone had seen him.

I knew I must have been looking absolutely crazed because people were looking at me askance. Some were even moving out of my way, as if I was some deranged gunman on the rampage.

Fortunately, not everyone reacted that way.

After about thirty yards, I asked a young girl who was walking down the road with a bag from the Apple store at the Oxford Street end of Regent Street. She'd obviously walked all the way down the street, so I asked her if she'd seen a cat.

'Oh yeah,' she said. 'I saw a cat weaving along

the street. Ginger. Had a lead hanging behind it. One bloke tried to stamp on the lead and catch it but the cat was too quick for him.'

My immediate reaction was joy. I could have kissed her. I just knew it was Bob. But that quickly gave way to paranoia. Who was that bloke who'd tried to catch him? What was he planning to do with him? Would that have frightened Bob even more? Was he now cowering somewhere where I'd never find him?

With all these new thoughts bouncing around in my head, I carried on down Regent Street, sticking my head into every shop I passed. Most of the shop assistants looked horrified to see this long-haired figure standing in their doorways and took a step back. Others just flashed me blank expressions and slow shakes of the head. I could see what they were thinking. They thought I was some piece of dirt that had just blown in off the street.

After about half a dozen shops, my mood began to swing again, this time back towards resignation. I had no idea how long it was since Bob had run off. Time had seemed to slow down. It was as if it was all happening in slow motion. I was close to giving up.

A couple of hundred yards down Regent Street, there was a side street ahead leading back down to Piccadilly. From there he could have headed in any one of a dozen directions: into Mayfair or even across the road down to St James's and Haymarket. If he'd gone that far then I knew he was lost.

I was about to give up and head down the side

street, when I stuck my head into a ladies' clothes shop. There were a couple of shop assistants there looking a bit perplexed and looking towards the back of the shop.

They turned to see me and the moment I said the word 'cat' their faces lit up.

'A ginger tom?' one of them said.

'Yes, he's got a collar and lead.'

'He's round the back here,' one of them said, gesturing for me to come in and shut the door.

'That's why we shut the door,' the other one said. 'We didn't want him to get run over.'

'We figured someone was looking for him because of the lead.'

They led me towards a row of open wardrobes filled with fancy-looking clothes. I noticed the prices on some of them. Each one cost more money than I'd make in a month. But then, in the corner of one of the wardrobes, curled up in a ball, I saw Bob.

As time had slowed down during the past few minutes, a part of me had wondered whether he was trying to get away from me. Maybe he'd had enough of me? Maybe he didn't want the life I offered him any more? So when I approached him I was prepared for him to bolt again and run off. But he didn't.

I'd barely whispered softly, 'Hey Bob, it's me', before he jumped straight into my arms.

All my fears about him wanting rid of me evaporated as he purred deeply and rubbed himself against me.

'You gave me such a scare there, mate,' I said, stroking him. 'I thought I'd lost you.'

I looked up and saw that the two shopkeepers were standing nearby watching. One of them was dabbing her eyes, close to tears.

'I'm so glad you found him,' she said. 'He looked like such a lovely cat. We were wondering what we'd do with him if no one showed up before closing time.'

She came closer and stroked Bob for a moment as well. We then chatted for a couple of minutes as she and her colleague got ready to close the till and started preparing to shut up shop for the evening.

'Bye, Bob,' the pair said as we headed off back into the throng around Piccadilly Circus with Bob perched on my shoulder again.

When I got back to Ripley's I discovered — to my mild amazement — that my guitar was still there. Maybe the security guy at the door had kept an eye on it. Or perhaps one of the community support officers in the area had made sure it was safe. At the time there was a mobile police unit next to us. All the police and community support people loved Bob. He had become very popular with the police. I had no idea who the Good Samaritan was but to be honest I didn't care. I was just glad that Bob and I were reunited.

I wasted no time in gathering up my stuff and calling it a night. We'd not made enough money but that wasn't my biggest concern. I stopped at a general store and, with most of the cash I had on me, bought myself a little belt clip that I attached, first to me then to his lead. It would make sure that we remained connected all the

111

time. On the bus rather than sitting on the seat next to me as usual, he sat on my lap. He could be an inscrutable chap but at other times I knew exactly what Bob was thinking. Tonight was one of those occasions. We were together, and neither of us wanted that to change.

10

Santa Paws

During those first few days and weeks after the drama at Piccadilly, Bob and I clung to each other like two survivors hanging on to a life raft at sea. We'd both been badly shaken by the incident.

It made me think long and hard about our friendship. For a while I kept wondering whether his escape had been a signal that he wanted to put some distance between us. Deep down I knew that if he wanted to go back on to the streets — or wherever it was he came from — ultimately there was nothing I could, or should, do to stop him.

I'd even thought through what I should do if he showed any sign of wanting to run away again. If he did, and I managed to catch him before he disappeared altogether, I decided I'd give him away to the RSPCA or Battersea Dogs and Cats Home where they had a really nice cattery. I didn't want to be his gaoler. He had been too good a friend to me for me to curtail his freedom. He didn't deserve that.

Thankfully though, it hadn't come to that.

Once or twice since the incident, he had elected not to go out with me. When I had got the harness out in the morning he had run behind the sofa or hid under the table to tell me he wasn't up for it. I'd left him to it. But in the main he had been happy to come out every day. And when he had, he had been a slightly different character, more attentive to me but, in a strange way, also more relaxed.

Despite what had happened at Piccadilly Circus, he wasn't as frightened in crowds as he had been occasionally in the past. Maybe this was because I now had him clipped to my belt and kept a tighter hold on his lead when he was out. The truth was that I think he felt closer to me now. Our bond had been put to the test — and survived. I got the impression that now he wanted to stay by my side more strongly than ever.

Of course, it hadn't all been a bed of roses; working on the streets of London, there are bound to be moments when you feel threatened. A couple of weeks after we saw that strange inflated character at Piccadilly we were in Covent Garden when we saw a troupe of street performers on giant stilts. They were old-fashioned French performance artists and had really, garish, scary faces.

The instant he saw them tottering around above our heads, I could tell Bob felt threatened. He squeezed in close to me. I was trying to concentrate on singing, but every now and again he stopped me from playing the guitar as he flopped his tail over the fret board.

'Cut it out, Bob,' I said, apologising to the one or two tourists who'd stopped to listen.

Of course, they thought it was funny and part of the act. If only I could manage to get Bob to do what I wanted so easily.

As soon as the figures on stilts had disappeared it was a completely different story, of course. With them gone he was relaxed again and he moved away from me slightly. It was as if he knew that I was his safety net. I was glad to provide it.

★   ★   ★

As Christmas 2007 approached and our first calendar year together drew to a close, our life had settled into a real routine. Each morning I'd get up to find him waiting patiently by his bowl in the kitchen. He'd guzzle down his breakfast then give himself a good wash, licking his paws and face clean. Bob was still very reluctant to do his toilet inside the flat and most mornings I'd take him downstairs to relieve himself. On other occasions I'd leave him out and let him find his own way out to the grass. He'd find his way down and back up again without any trouble. I'd then get ready, pack up my rucksack, grab my guitar and head into town.

With Christmas only days away, the crowds in Covent Garden were getting bigger and bigger. So too were the number of treats and gifts Bob was getting. From the very early days, people had got into the habit of giving Bob little presents.

The first one came from a middle-aged lady who worked in an office not far from James Street and would regularly stop and talk to us. She'd had a ginger tom herself many years earlier and had told me that Bob reminded her of him.

She had arrived one evening with a big grin on her face and a smart bag from a fancy pet shop. 'I hope you don't mind but I bought Bob a little present,' she said.

'Of course not,' I said.

'It's not much,' she said, fishing out a little stuffed figure of a mouse.

'It's got a little catnip in it,' she smiled. 'Not a lot, don't worry.'

There was a part of me that felt awkward about it. Catnip was, after all, addictive to cats. I'd read all sorts of stuff about how it can drive them crazy if they get hooked on it. It was bad enough with me trying desperately to straighten myself out. I didn't want Bob developing a habit as well.

But she was too nice a lady to disappoint her. She stayed for a little while, relishing the sight of seeing Bob playing with the little mouse.

As the weather took a turn for the worse, people began to give Bob more practical presents.

One day another lady, a striking-looking Russian, sidled up to us smiling.

'Hope you don't mind, but with the weather turning cold, I thought I'd knit Bob something to keep him warm,' she said, producing a beautiful, light-blue knitted scarf from her shoulder bag.

'Wow,' I said, genuinely taken aback. 'That's great.'

I immediately wrapped it around Bob's neck.

It fitted perfectly and looked fantastic. The lady was over the moon. She reappeared a week or two later with a matching blue waistcoat. I was no fashion expert, as anyone who met me would have been able to tell in an instant, but even I could tell that Bob looked amazing in it. People were soon queuing to take photographs of him in it. I should have charged; I would have made a fortune.

Since then at least half a dozen more people — well, women — had dropped off various items of knitted clothing for Bob.

One lady had even embroidered the name Bob into the little scarf that she had created for him. It struck me one day that Bob was becoming a fashion model. He was regularly modelling some new creation a kindly soul had made for him. It gave a new meaning to the word 'catwalk'.

It just underlined what I'd realised already: that I wasn't the only one who was forming a deep affection for Bob. He seemed to make friends with almost everyone he met. It was a gift I wished I had myself. I'd never found it that easy to bond with people.

No one had fallen more deeply in love with Bob than my ex-girlfriend Belle. We were still close friends, probably better friends than when we were together and she would pop round to the flat on a regular basis. It was partly to see me and hang out but I was pretty sure that she was also coming over to see Bob.

The two of them would play together for hours on the sofa. Bob thought the world of her, I could tell.

It was about three weeks before Christmas that she came round with a plastic shopping bag in her hand and a big grin on her face.

'What have you got in there?' I said, sensing she was up to something.

'It's not for you, it's for Bob,' she said, teasing me.

Bob was sitting in his usual spot under the radiator, but perked up the minute he heard his name mentioned.

'Bob, come here, I've got a surprise for you,' Belle said, flopping on to the sofa with the bag. He was soon padding over, curious to find out what was inside.

Belle pulled out a couple of small animal T-shirts. One just had a picture of a cute-looking kitten on it. But the other one was red with green trim on it. It had the words 'Santa Paws' in large white letters with a big paw print underneath it.

'Oh, that's really cool Bob, isn't it?' I said. 'That's the perfect thing to wear when we're in Covent Garden close to Christmas. That will really put a smile on people's faces.'

It certainly did that.

I don't know if it was the Christmas spirit or simply seeing him in his outfit, but the effect was amazing.

'Ah, look it's Santa Paws,' I'd hear people say almost every few minutes.

A lot of people would stop and drop a bit of silver into my guitar case, others, however, wanted to give Bob something.

On one occasion this very well-heeled lady

stopped and started cooing over Bob.

'He's fabulous,' she said. 'What would he like for Christmas?'

'I don't know, madam,' I replied.

'Well, put it this way, what does he need?' she said.

'He could do with a spare harness, I guess. Or something to keep him warm when the weather gets really cold. Or just get him some toys. Everybody likes toys at Christmas.'

'Jolly good,' she said, getting up and leaving.

I didn't think much more of it, but then, about an hour later, the lady reappeared. She had a big grin on her face and was carrying a smart-looking hand-knitted stocking, with cat designs on the front. I looked inside and could see it was stuffed with goodies: food, toys and stuff.

'You must promise me that you won't open it till Christmas,' she said. 'You must keep it under your tree until Christmas morning.'

I didn't have the heart to tell her that I didn't have enough money for a Christmas tree or any decorations in the flat. The best I'd been able to rustle up was a USB Christmas tree that plugged into the battered old Xbox I'd recently found at a charity shop.

In the days after that, however, I made a decision. She was right. I should have a decent Christmas for once. I had something to celebrate. I had Bob.

I suppose I'd become desensitised to Christmas because I hadn't had a decent one in years. I was one of those people who actively dreaded it.

During the past decade or so I'd spent most of them at places like Shelter, where they did a big Christmas lunch for homeless people. It was all very well meaning and I'd had a laugh or two there. But it just reminded me of what I didn't have: a normal life and a normal family. It just reminded me that I'd cocked up my life.

Once or twice I'd spent it on my own, trying to forget the fact that my family was on the other side of the world. Well, most of it. On a couple of occasions, I'd spent the day with my father. After going missing for a year when I first ended up on the streets, I'd stayed in contact, calling him very occasionally and he'd invited me down to his house in south London. But it hadn't been the greatest of experiences. He didn't really think much of me. I couldn't really blame him. I wasn't exactly a son to be proud about.

I'd been grateful for a nice lunch and a few drinks and, most of all, a bit of company. But it hadn't really been a great success and we hadn't done it again.

This year was different though. I invited Belle round on Christmas Eve for a drink. Then for Christmas Day I splashed out on a ready-made turkey breast with all the trimmings. I wasn't really into cooking and didn't have the equipment even if I had been. I got Bob some really nice treats including his favourite chicken meal.

When Christmas Day arrived we got up reasonably early and went out for a short walk so that Bob could do his business. There were other families from the block heading off to see

120

relatives and friends. We all exchanged 'Happy Christmases' and smiles. Even that was more than I'd experienced in a long while.

Back up at the flat, I gave Bob his stocking. He had spotted it days earlier and had obviously guessed it was meant for him. I emptied the contents one by one. There were treats, toys, balls, and little soft things containing catnip. He absolutely loved it and was soon playing with his new toys like an excitable child on Christmas morning. It was pretty adorable.

I cooked our lunch early in the afternoon, then put a hat on each of us, had a can of beer and watched television for the rest of the afternoon and evening. It was the best Christmas I'd had in years.

11

Mistaken Identity

By the spring and summer of 2008, being a busker on the streets of London was becoming more and more difficult, almost impossible at times.

There were a couple of reasons. I know people assume the economy doesn't affect people on the streets, but that's not the case at all. The recession — which at that point was only just gearing up — had hit me and people in my position quite hard. The kind-hearted folk who used to think nothing of dropping me and Bob a pound or two, were now holding on to their money. One or two regulars even told me as much. They said they were worried about losing their jobs. I couldn't really argue with them. So, as a result, I was having to work much longer hours often to make less money to feed me and Bob and keep us warm.

I could live with that, the bigger problem was the fact that the authorities had started coming down hard on street performers who didn't work in the designated spots. I wasn't sure why they'd decided to do this, especially now, but I did know that it had begun to make my life a real headache.

Most of the Covent Guardians had always been reasonable. I'd had trouble from the most aggressive of them, but in general they'd never been really heavy with me. But even they had started confiscating stuff if they felt you weren't taking what they said seriously. I don't think they had any new powers, they had just been told to get a bit more serious about what they were doing.

There were also a few, new faces among them. One of the more aggressive of the newcomers had threatened to take away my guitar a couple of times. I'd managed to dissuade him by promising to play in a designated area — or move out of the neighbourhood. I'd then sneaked around the corner for half an hour before returning to James Street.

It had become a constant game of hide and seek, but I was running out of places to hide. The new Guardians seemed to know where I was going to be. Most days now I'd be moved along or spoken to at some point. It was wearing me down. Deep down I knew that my time as a busker was drawing to an end. The straw that broke the camel's back came one afternoon in May that year.

Another of the reasons busking had become particularly hard for me was the staff at Covent Garden tube station. The bad vibe I'd been getting from there had become more and more unpleasant. I don't know why but they didn't want me busking there. There were now a number of ticket inspectors who would regularly wander across the road from the entrance to the tube station and give me a real mouthful of abuse.

I could handle that. I was well used to it. But they'd definitely been talking about me together and had come up with some kind of plan to campaign against me. Every now and again they would call up the British Transport Police, who would turn up and give me hassle. As if I needed any more of that. I'd learned to deal with them in the same way as the other authorities: I'd slope off, promising never to darken their doorstep again, then slink back into position when the coast was clear. I saw no harm in what I was doing. No one was getting hurt were they?

All that changed one afternoon.

★   ★   ★

I'd headed into Covent Garden as usual with Bob. I had a friend staying with me at the time, a guy called Dylan, who I'd met way back when I was with the band. He'd been kicked out of his previous accommodation when he'd refused to pay an extortionate new rent by some unscrupulous landlord. He needed a floor to sleep on for a couple of weeks. I'd been there myself, so I couldn't refuse him. He had begun sleeping on my sofa.

Bob hadn't taken too kindly to Dylan's arrival at first. I think he felt he was going to lose out in my affections. But as soon as he realised that Dylan was, in fact, another animal lover, and discovered that he was going to get more attention, then he was fine. Bob thrived on attention.

This particular afternoon Dylan decided he

was going to come into London with us and hang around Covent Garden. It was a lovely, sunny day and he felt like enjoying it. He was playing with Bob as I set myself up on the corner of James Street. Looking back on it, I can't believe how fortunate it was that he was there.

I'd barely put the guitar strap over my shoulder when a British Transport Police van arrived at speed and pulled up alongside the pavement. Three officers jumped out and immediately started walking towards me.

'What's all this about?' Dylan said.

'Don't know. More of the usual stuff,' I said, fully expecting to have to go through the usual tap dance of promising to move away.

I was wrong.

'Right you, you're coming with us,' one of the officers said, pointing at me.

'What for?' I said.

'We're arresting you on suspicion of using threatening behaviour.'

'What? Threatening who? I don't know what the hell — '

Before I could finish my sentence they had grabbed me. While one of them read me my rights, another one stuck me in handcuffs.

'We'll explain at the station. Let's get your shit together and get in the van before we make things even worse for you,' he said.

'What about my cat?' I said gesturing at Bob.

'We've got some dog kennels at the station, we'll stick him in there,' another of the officers said. 'Unless you've got someone to take him.'

My head was spinning. I had no idea what was

happening. But then, out of the corner of my eye, I saw Dylan. He was looking sheepish and didn't want to get involved.

'Dylan, will you look after Bob?' I said. 'Take him back to the flat. The keys are in my rucksack.'

He nodded and started moving towards Bob. I watched him scoop him up and reassure him. I could see the look on Bob's face; he was terrified by what was happening to me. Through the mesh windows at the back of the van, I watched as the figures of Dylan and Bob standing on the pavement disappeared from view.

We drove to the British Transport Police station. I still had no idea what was going on.

Within a few minutes I was standing in front of a desk clerk being asked to empty all my pockets and to answer all sorts of questions. I was then led into a cell where I was told to wait until I was seen by an officer. As I sat there in the barren cell, the walls gouged with graffiti and the floors smelling of stale urine, it brought awful memories flooding back.

I'd had run-ins with the police before, mostly for petty theft.

When you are homeless or have a drug habit you try to find easy options to make money. And, to be honest, few things are easier than shoplifting. My main thing was stealing meat. I'd lift legs of lamb and expensive steaks. Jamie Oliver steaks. Lamb shanks. Gammon joints. Never chicken, chicken is too low value. What I stole was the stuff with the highest price value. What you get is half the price on the label. If you go to a pub and sell the stuff that's what you could expect to get. Pubs are very solid ground for selling stolen goods. Everybody knows that.

The first time I did it to pay for my habit was in 2001 or 2002, something like that. Before that I'd been begging to feed my habit. Before *that* I'd been on a methadone course. I'd got clean but then I'd started using again because things were bad. I'd been moved into some dodgy accommodation where everyone was using and had spiralled back into bad habits.

I can still remember the first time I got busted. It was at the Marks and Spencer's at the Angel, Islington. I used to dress up smartly and tie my hair back, dress like a postman at the end of his daily rounds popping in for a snack or a pint of milk on the way home. It was all about appearance. You had to be clever about it. If I'd walked in with a rucksack or a shopping bag I'd never have stood a chance. I carried a postman's Royal Mail bag around with me. It's different today but back then nobody looked twice at you if you had one of those bags slung over your shoulders.

Anyhow, I got stopped one day. I had about one hundred and twenty pounds' worth of meat on me.

I was taken into police custody. At that time they gave me an on-the-spot fine of eight pounds for theft. I was lucky to get that because it was my first time.

Of course, it didn't stop me. I had a habit. I had to do what I had to do. I was on heroin and an occasional bit of crack. You take the risk. You have to.

When you get nicked it sucks. But you have got to bite the bullet. Obviously, you sit there feeling sorry for yourself, but you aren't going to fight the powers that be.

You try to get out of it, you make up lies but they don't believe you. They never really do. It's a vicious circle when you are down.

That was why busking had been so good for me. It was legal. It kept me straight. But now here I was back in the nick. It felt like a real kick in the stomach.

★　★　★

I'd been in the cell for about half an hour when the door opened suddenly and a white-shirted officer ushered me out.

'Come on,' he said.

'Where are you taking me now?' I asked.

'You'll see,' he said.

I was taken into a bare room with a few plastic chairs and a single table.

There were a couple of officers sitting opposite me. They looked disinterested, to be honest. But then one of them started questioning me.

'Where were you yesterday evening at around 6.30p.m.?' one of them asked.

'Um, I was busking in Covent Garden,' I said.

'Where?'

'On the corner of James Street, opposite the entrance to the tube,' I said, which was true.

'Did you go into the tube station at any time that evening?' the copper asked.

'No, I never go in there,' I said. 'I travel by bus.'

'Well, how come we've got at least two witnesses saying that you were in the station and that you verbally abused and spat at a female ticket attendant?'

'I've got absolutely no idea,' I said, bemused.

'They saw you come up the escalator from the tube and try to go through the automatic barrier without a ticket.'

'Well, as I say, that can't have been me,' I said.

'When you were challenged you verbally abused a female member of staff.'

I just sat there shaking my head. This was surreal.

'You were then led to the ticket booth and asked to buy a ticket,' he went on. 'When you did so, against your will, you then spat at the window of the ticket booth.'

That was it; I lost my cool.

'Look, this is bullshit,' I said. 'I told you I wasn't in the tube station last night. I'm never in there. And I never travel by tube. Me and my cat travel everywhere by bus.'

They just looked at me as if I was telling the biggest lies in the world.

They asked me if I wanted to make a statement, so I did, explaining that I'd been busking all night. I knew the CCTV footage would back this up. But at the back of my mind I was having all sorts of paranoid thoughts.

What if this was all a fit up? What if they had doctored the CCTV footage in the tube station? What if it went to court and it was my word against three or four London Underground officers?

Worst of all, I found myself anxiously wondering what would happen to Bob. Who would look after him? Would he stay with them or head back on to the street? And what would happen to him there? Thinking about it did my head in.

They kept me in for about another two or three hours. After a while I lost all track of time. There was no natural light in the room so I had no idea whether it was day or night outside. At one point a lady police officer came in, with a surly-looking male officer behind her.

'I need to do a DNA test,' she said as he took a position in the corner where he stood with his arms folded, glaring at me.

'OK,' I said, ignoring him. I figured I had nothing to lose. 'What do I have to do?' I asked the female officer.

'Just sit there and I'll take a swab of saliva from your mouth,' she said.

She produced a little kit, with loads of swabs and test tubes.

Suddenly I felt like I was at the dentist.

'Open wide,' she said.

She then stuck a long, cotton bud into my mouth, gave it a bit of a scrape around the inside of my cheek and that was that.

'All done,' she said, putting the bud in a test tube and packing her stuff away.

Eventually, I was let out of the cell and taken back to the desk at the front of the station where I signed for my stuff. I had to sign a form saying that I was released on bail and told that I had to return a couple of days later.

'When will I know if I am being formally charged?' I asked the duty officer, suspecting that he couldn't really tell me that. To my surprise he said that I'd probably know when I came back in a couple of days' time.

'Really?' I said.

'More than likely,' he said.

That was good and bad, I decided immediately. Good in the sense that I'd not have to wait months to find out if I was going to be charged, bad in the sense that if they were going to charge me I could find myself spending time inside very soon.

I really didn't relish that prospect.

★   ★   ★

After finally being let free, I emerged into the streets behind Warren Street in pitch darkness. There were already little groups of homeless people hunkering down for the night, hiding themselves away in alleyways.

It was approaching eleven o'clock. By the time I got back to Seven Sisters tube station it was close to midnight and the streets were full of drunks and people being turfed out of the pubs.

I breathed a huge sigh of relief when I got inside the flat.

Dylan was watching television with Bob curled up in his usual spot under the radiator. The minute I walked through the door, he jumped up and padded over to me, tilting his head to one side and looking up at me.

'Hello, mate, you all right?' I said, dropping to

131

my knees and stroking him.

He immediately clambered up on to my knee and started rubbing against my face.

Dylan had headed off into the kitchen but soon reappeared with a cold tin of lager from the fridge.

'That's a life saver, thanks,' I said, ripping the ring off the tin and taking a slug of cold beer.

I sat up for a couple of hours with Dylan, trying to make sense of what had happened to me. I knew the ticket collectors at Covent Garden tube didn't like me — but I didn't think they'd go so far as to try and frame me for a crime I didn't commit.

'There's no way they can fix the DNA to match yours, mate,' Dylan reassured me.

I wish I could have been so certain.

I slept fitfully that night. I'd been really shaken by the experience. No matter how much I tried to tell myself it would work out fine, I couldn't erase the thought that my life could be about to take a terrible turn. I felt powerless, angry — and really scared.

★ ★ ★

I decided to give Covent Garden a wide berth the following day. Bob and I played around Neal Street and one or two other places towards Tottenham Court Road. But my heart wasn't in it. I was too worried about what was going to happen when I turned up at the police station the following day. Again that night I struggled to get much sleep.

I was due to report at the Transport Police station at midday but set off early to make sure I was on time. I didn't want to give them any excuses. I left Bob back at home — just in case I was going to be kept there for hours again. He had picked up on my anxiety as I'd paced around the flat eating my toast at breakfast.

'Don't worry, mate, I'll be back before you know it,' I reassured him as I left. If only I'd been as confident of that as I sounded.

It took me a while to find the station, which was hidden away on a backstreet off Tottenham Court Road. I'd arrived there in the back of a van and left after dark, so it wasn't surprising that I had trouble finding it.

When I did locate it, I had to sit and hang around for twenty minutes, during which time I found it hard to concentrate on anything. I was eventually called into a room where a couple of officers were waiting for me, one man and a younger woman.

They had files in front of them, which looked ominous. I wondered what they'd dug up about my past. God only knows what skeletons were hiding in that particular cupboard.

The male officer was the first to speak. He told me that I wasn't going to be charged with the offence of using threatening behaviour. I guessed why that was.

'The DNA didn't match the saliva on the ticket collector's booth did it?' I said, feeling suddenly empowered by what he'd told me.

He just looked at me with a tight-lipped smile. He couldn't say anything; I knew that. But he didn't need to. It seemed obvious to me that someone at the tube station had tried to fit me up, but had failed.

If that was the good news, the bad news wasn't long in following.

The lady told me that I was being charged with illegally busking, or 'touting for reward', to give it its formal title.

They shoved a piece of paper towards me and told me I was to report to court in a week's time.

I left the station relieved. 'Touting for reward' was a relatively minor offence, certainly compared to threatening behaviour. If I was lucky I'd get away with a small fine and a rap across the knuckles, nothing more.

Threatening behaviour would have been a completely different matter, of course. That would have left me open to a heavy punishment, maybe even imprisonment. I'd got off lightly.

Part of me wanted to fight back at the injustice of what had happened to me. The description of the person who spat on the window bore no relation to my appearance. I held on to the paperwork and thought I could do them for wrongful arrest.

But, to be honest, the main thought in my mind as I headed home that afternoon was relief and a sense that I'd turned some sort of corner. I wasn't sure yet what it was.

⋆ ⋆ ⋆

I still had to get past the court hearing. I went to the local Citizens Advice centre and got a bit of legal advice. I should probably have done that earlier, but I'd been too messed up to think of it.

It turned out that because I was on a drug rehab programme and living in sheltered accommodation, I was eligible for legal aid. But the truth was I didn't think I needed a solicitor representing me in court, so I simply got some advice about what to say.

It was pretty straightforward. I needed to front up and admit that I was guilty of busking: plain and simple. I simply had to go along, plead accordingly and hope the magistrate wasn't some kind of sadist with a hatred for street musicians.

When the day came I put on a clean shirt (over the top of a T-shirt bearing the slogan 'Extremely Unhappy') and had a shave before heading to court. The waiting area was full of all sorts of people, from some really scary-looking guys with shaven heads and Eastern European accents to a couple of middle-aged guys in grey suits who were up on driving offences.

'James Bowen. The court calls Mr James Bowen,' a plummy-sounding voice eventually announced. I took a deep breath and headed in.

The magistrates looked at me like I was a piece of dirt that had been blown in off the street. But under the law there wasn't too much they could do to me, especially as it was my first offence for busking.

I got a three-month conditional discharge. I wasn't fined.

But they made it clear that if I did reoffend I could face a fine — and even worse.

Belle and Bob were waiting for me outside the courthouse after the hearing was over. Bob immediately jumped off her lap and walked over to me. He didn't want to be too melodramatic about it all, but it was clear he was pleased to see me.

'How did it go?' Belle asked.

'Three-month conditional discharge, but if I get caught again I'm for the high jump,' I said.

'So what are you going to do?' she said.

I looked at her, then looked down at Bob. The answer must have been written all over my face.

I had reached the end of the road. I'd been busking on and off now for almost a decade. Times had changed — and my life had changed, certainly since Bob had come into it. So it was becoming more and more clear to me that I couldn't carry on busking, it didn't make any sense on any level. There were times when it didn't earn me enough money to make ends meet. There were times when it put me — and more importantly, Bob — in dangerous situations. And now there was a real danger that if I was caught busking in the wrong place again, I could get banged up in prison. It just wasn't worth it.

'I don't know what I'm going to do, Belle,' I said. 'But the one thing I know I'm not going to do is carry on busking.'

12

Number 683

My head was spinning for the next few days. I felt a real mixture of emotions.

Part of me was still angry at the unfairness of what had happened. I felt like I'd lost my livelihood simply because a few people had taken against me. At the same time, however, another part of me had begun to see it might have been a blessing in disguise.

Deep down I knew I couldn't carry on busking all my life. I wasn't going to turn my life around singing Johnny Cash and Oasis songs on street corners. I wasn't going to build up the strength to get myself totally clean by relying on my guitar. It began to dawn on me that I was at a big crossroads, that I had an opportunity to put the past behind me. I'd been there before, but for the first time in years, I felt like I was ready to take it.

That was all very well in theory, of course. I also knew the brutal truth: my options were pretty limited. How was I now going to earn money? No one was going to give me a job.

It wasn't because I was stupid; I knew that. Thanks to the IT work I'd done when I was a teenager back in Australia I was fairly knowledgeable when it came to computers. I spent as much time as I could on friends' laptops or on

137

the free computers at the local library and had taught myself a fair bit about the subject. But I didn't have any references or relevant experience in the UK to rely on and when a prospective employer asked me where I'd spent the past ten years I couldn't exactly say I'd been working for Google or Microsoft. So I had to forget that.

There wasn't even any point in me applying to do a training course in computing because they wouldn't accept me. Officially I was still on a drug rehabilitation programme. I was living in sheltered accommodation and didn't even have an O level to my name. They wouldn't — and probably couldn't — touch me with a bargepole. All in all, I was a non-starter when it came to getting a normal job. Whatever normal is.

I realised quickly that there was only one realistic alternative. I didn't have the luxury of being able to wait for something to turn up. I needed to make money to look after myself and Bob. So a couple of days after the court hearing I set off with Bob for Covent Garden — for the first time in years, without my guitar on my back. When I got to the piazza I headed straight for the spot where I knew I'd probably find a girl called Sam, the area's *Big Issue* coordinator.

I had tried selling the *Big Issue* before, back in 1998 and 1999 when I first ended up on the streets. I'd got myself accredited and worked the streets around Charing Cross and Trafalgar Square. It hadn't worked out. I'd lasted less than a year before I gave it up.

I could still remember how difficult it was. When I was selling the *Big Issue*, so many people used to come up to me and snarl 'get a job'. That used to really upset me. They didn't realise that selling the *Big Issue* is a job. In fact, being a *Big Issue* seller effectively means you are running your own business. When I was selling the magazine I had overheads. I had to buy copies to sell. So each day I turned up at the coordinator's stand I had to have at least a few quid in order to buy a few copies of the magazine. That old saying is as true for *Big Issue* sellers as it is for anyone else: you have to have money, to make money.

So many people think it's a complete charity job and that they give the magazines to the sellers for free. That's just not the case. If it was, people would be selling a lot more than they do. The *Big Issue* philosophy is that it is helping people to help themselves. But back then I wasn't really sure I wanted any help. I wasn't ready for it.

I could still remember some of the grim, soul-destroying days I'd spent sitting on a wet and windy street-corner pitch trying to coax and cajole Londoners to part with their cash in return for a magazine. It was really hard, especially as back then my life was still ruled by drugs. All I usually got for my trouble was a load of abuse or a kick in the ribs.

Most of all it had been hard because I had been invisible. Most people just didn't give me the time of day. They would do all they could to avoid me, in fact. That's why I had turned to busking, at least then I had my music to attract people's attention and let them know I was actually a living, breathing creature. And even then most of them ignored me.

I wouldn't have even contemplated going back to selling the *Big Issue* if it hadn't been for Bob. The way he'd transformed my fortunes — and my spirits — on the streets had been amazing. If I could do as well selling the *Big Issue* as I'd done busking with Bob then maybe I could take that big step forward. Of course there was only one problem: I had to get them to accept me first.

I found Sam at the spot where the area's *Big Issue* sellers gathered to buy their magazines, on a side street off the main piazza of Covent Garden. There were a few vendors there, all men. I recognised one or two of the faces. One of them was a guy called Steve, who I knew was a driver for the magazine. I'd seen him around the place, delivering the magazines on Mondays when the new issues came out.

We'd registered each other's presence around Covent Garden a couple of times and were a bit wary of each other. I got the distinct impression he wasn't very pleased to see me, but I didn't care. I hadn't come to see him; it was Sam I needed to talk to.

'Hello, you two not busking today?' she said, recognising me and Bob and giving him a friendly pat.

'No, I'm going to have to knock that on the head,' I said. 'Bit of trouble with the cops. If I get caught doing it illegally again I'm going to be in big trouble. Can't risk it now I've got Bob to look after. Can I, mate?'

'OK,' Sam said, her face immediately signalling that she could see what was coming next.

'So,' I said, rocking up and down on my heels. 'I was wondering — '

Sam smiled and cut me off. 'Well, it all depends on whether you meet the criteria,' she said.

'Oh yeah, I do,' I said, knowing that as a person in what was known as 'vulnerable housing' I was eligible to sell the magazine.

'But you are going to have to go through all the red tape and go down to Vauxhall to sign up,' she said.

'Right.'

'You know where the offices are?' she said, reaching for a card.

'Not sure,' I said. I was sure the offices had been somewhere else when I'd signed up years ago.

'Get a bus to Vauxhall and get off by the train station. It's across the road from there not far from the river on the one-way system,' she said. 'Once you're badged up, just come back here and see me and we can get you going.'

I took the card and headed home with Bob. 'Better get ourselves organised, Bob,' I said. 'We're going for a job interview.'

I needed to get some paperwork sorted before I could go to the *Big Issue* office, so the next day I went to see my housing worker. In any case, I was supposed to see her regularly. I explained my current situation and what had happened with the Transport Police. She happily gave me a letter saying that I was living in 'vulnerable housing' and that selling the *Big Issue* would be a good way of helping me get my life back together again.

The day after that I made myself look respectable, got my hair tied back, put on a decent shirt and set off for Vauxhall with all the bits and pieces I needed.

I also took Bob with me. Part of my thinking was that Bob might help me sell magazines in the way that he'd helped me make money busking. He was going to be part of my team, so I wanted to get him registered as well, if that was at all possible.

The *Big Issue* offices are in an ordinary-looking office block on the south side of the Thames, near Vauxhall Bridge and the MI6 building.

The first thing I noticed when I arrived in the reception area was a large sign saying 'No Dogs Allowed'. Apparently they used to allow dogs in there but they had banned them as so many dogs had started fighting with each other. It didn't say anything about cats, however.

After filling in a few bits of paper, I was told to take a seat and wait. After a while I was called in to have an interview with a guy in one of the offices. He was a decent bloke and we chatted for a while. He'd been on the streets himself years ago and had used the *Big Issue* as a stepping-stone to help get his life together.

I explained my circumstances. He was sympathetic.

'I know what it's like out there, James, believe me,' he said.

It took just a few minutes before he gave me a thumbs-up sign and told me to go and get badged up in another office.

I had to have my photo taken and then wait to get a laminated badge with my vendor number on it. I asked the guy who was issuing the badges whether Bob could have an ID card as well.

'Sorry,' he said, shaking his head. 'Pets aren't allowed to have their own badges. We've had this before with dogs. Never with a cat, though.'

'Well, what about if he is in the picture with me?' I asked.

He pulled a face, as if to say, I'm not sure about that. But in the end he relented.

'Go on then,' he said.

'Smile, Bob,' I said, as we sat in front of the camera.

As he waited for the photo to be processed, the guy got on with the rest of the registration process. When you become a *Big Issue* seller you get assigned a random number. They are not issued in sequence. If they did that the numbers would now be running into the thousands because so many people have signed up to sell the *Big Issue* over the years then just disappeared off the face of the earth. So when someone fails to show up on the records for a while the number comes back into circulation. They have to do that.

After waiting about a quarter of an hour, the guy reappeared at the desk.

'Here you go, Mr Bowen,' he said, handing me the laminated badge.

I couldn't help breaking into a big grin at the

143

picture. Bob was on the left-hand side. We were a team. *Big Issue* Vendors Number 683.

★ ★ ★

It was a long journey back to Tottenham, involving two buses. So I whiled away the hour and a half it took us reading through the little booklet they gave me. I'd read something similar ten years earlier but hadn't really retained any of it. If I was honest, I'd not really taken it seriously. I'd been too out of it a lot of the time. This time around I was determined to take it more seriously.

It began with the magazine's main philosophy:

'The *Big Issue* exists to offer homeless and vulnerably housed people the opportunity to earn a legitimate income by selling a magazine to the general public. We believe in offering 'a hand up, not a hand out' and in enabling individuals to take control of their lives.'

That's exactly what I want, I said to myself, *a hand up. And this time I'll accept it.*

The next bit stated that I had to 'undergo an induction process and sign up to the code of conduct'. I knew the first bit meant that I'd have to work at a 'trial pitch', where my performance would be watched and assessed by the local organisers.

If that went well I'd be allocated a fixed pitch, it went on. I'd also get ten free copies of the magazine to get me started. It made it clear that it was then down to me. 'Once they have sold these magazines they can purchase further copies, which they buy for £1 and sell for £2, thereby making £1 per copy.'

The rules went on to explain that vendors were employed by the *Big Issue*. 'We do not reimburse them for magazines which they fail to sell, hence each individual must manage their sales and finances carefully. These skills, along with the confidence and self-esteem they build through selling the magazine, are crucial in helping homeless people reintegrate into mainstream society.'

That was the simple economics of it. But there was a lot more to it than that, as I would soon discover.

★   ★   ★

The next morning I headed back down to Covent Garden to see Sam, the coordinator. I was keen to get on with my 'induction'.

'All go OK down at Vauxhall?' she said, as Bob and I approached her.

'I guess it must have done. They gave me one of these,' I grinned, proudly producing my laminated badge from under my coat.

'Great,' Sam said, smiling at the photo of me and Bob. 'I'd better get you started then.'

She began by counting out my ten free copies of the magazine.

'There you go,' she said. 'You know you'll have to buy them after this?'

'Yep, I understand,' I said.

For a few minutes she studied a sheet of papers.

'Just trying to work out where to put your trial

pitch,' she said, apologetically.

A moment or two later I could see she'd made up her mind.

'Found somewhere?' I asked, feeling quite excited about it.

'Think so,' Sam said.

I couldn't believe what she said next.

'OK, we'll give you the training pitch just here,' she said, pointing in the direction of Covent Garden tube station, a few yards further up James Street.

I couldn't stop myself from bursting out laughing.

'Are you OK? Is that a problem?' she said, looking confused. 'I can look to see if there's somewhere else.'

'No, it's not a problem at all,' I said. 'It'll be great there. It'll be a real walk down memory lane. I'll get started right away.'

I wasted no time and set up immediately. It was mid-morning, a few hours before I'd normally have set up busking, but there were lots of people milling around, mostly tourists. It was a bright, sunny morning, which, I knew from experience, always puts people in a better and more generous mood.

When I'd been busking I'd always felt like I was running the gauntlet of the authorities by playing here. Selling the *Big Issue* was a totally different prospect. I was officially licensed to be there. So I placed myself as close to the station as possible without actually being inside the concourse.

I couldn't resist looking inside to see if there was any sign of the ticket officers who'd given

146

me grief in the past. Sure enough, I saw one of them, a big, sweaty fat guy in a blue shirt. He was too tied up to notice me at this stage but I knew that he would at some point.

In the meantime, I got on with the job of trying to shift my ten copies of the *Big Issue*.

I knew they'd given me this pitch because, as far as normal *Big Issue* sellers were concerned, it was a nightmare. The entrance and exit of a tube station is not a place where people usually have the time to slow down and engage with someone trying to sell them something. They are in a hurry, they have got places to go, people to see. A normal *Big Issue* seller would have done well to stop one in every thousand people that raced past him or her. It would have been a thankless task. During my time busking across the street, I'd spent enough time watching a succession of vendors try and fail to catch people's attention there to know the reality.

But I also knew that I wasn't a normal *Big Issue* seller. I had a secret weapon, one that had already cast his spell on Covent Garden. And he was soon weaving his magic.

★　★　★

I'd put Bob down on the pavement next to me where he was sitting contentedly watching the world go by. A lot of people didn't notice him as they flew past on their mobile phones, fishing inside their pockets for their tickets. But a lot of people did.

Within moments of me setting up, a couple of

young American tourists had pulled up to a halt and started pointing at Bob.

'Aaaah,' one of them said, immediately reaching for her camera.

'Do you mind if we take a picture of your cat?' the other one asked.

'Sure, why not?' I said, pleased that, unlike so many people, they'd had the decency to ask. 'Would you like to buy a copy of the *Big Issue* while you're at it. It will help him and me get some dinner tonight.'

'Oh sure,' the second girl said, looking almost ashamed that she'd not thought of it.

'It's no problem if you don't have the money,' I said. 'It's not compulsory.'

But before I could say anything else she'd given me a five-pound note.

'Oh, I'm not sure I've got any change. I've literally just started,' I said, feeling flustered myself now. I know a lot of people think *Big Issue* sellers routinely say this, but I genuinely didn't have much in my pockets. When I counted it out, I had just under a pound in shrapnel in my pocket and handed that over to her.

'That's fine,' she said. 'Keep the change and buy your cat something nice to eat.'

As the American girls left, another group of tourists passed by, this time Germans. Again, they started cooing over Bob. They didn't buy a magazine, but it didn't matter.

I knew already that I'd have no trouble selling the ten copies. In fact, I might even be heading back to Sam for some more stock before the end of the day.

Sure enough I sold six copies within the first hour. Most people gave me the correct money but one elderly gent in a smart, tweed suit, gave me a fiver. I was already feeling vindicated in making this move. I knew I wouldn't always fare this well and that there would be ups and downs. But I already felt like I'd taken a big step in a new direction.

It had been a pretty good day already, but the icing on the cake came after I'd been there for about two and a half hours. By now I was down to my last two magazines. I was suddenly aware of a bit of a commotion inside the station. All of a sudden a small group of London Underground staff appeared in the concourse in full view of me. They seemed to be deep in conversation about something and one or two of them were on walkie-talkies.

My mind couldn't help going back to what had recently happened to me. I wondered whether there had been another incident and whether some other poor sap was going to be fitted up for a crime that he hadn't committed.

Whatever the panic was, however, it soon passed and they began to disperse. It was then that the large, sweaty figure of the ticket attendant spotted me and Bob outside the station. He immediately marched in our direction.

He looked hassled and hot tempered and was as red as a beetroot in the face. They say that revenge is a dish best eaten cold, so I decided to stay cool.

'What the f*** are you doing here?' he said. 'I thought you'd been locked up. You know you're

149

not supposed to be here.'

I didn't say anything at first. Instead, very slowly and deliberately, I flashed him my *Big Issue* badge.

'I'm just doing my job, mate,' I said, savouring the mixture of bewilderment and anger that immediately began spreading across his face. 'I suggest you get on with yours.'

13

Pitch Perfect

I hadn't got many decisions right in my life. Whenever I'd been given an opportunity in the past ten years I'd screwed things up big time. Within a couple of days of deciding to become a *Big Issue* seller, however, I was pretty sure that I'd taken a step in the right direction for once.

It had an immediate impact on life for me and Bob. For a start it gave us more structure. I effectively had a Monday to Friday job, well, a Monday to Saturday one, in fact.

For those first two weeks, Bob and I worked at Covent Garden from Monday to Saturday, which tied in with the publication of the magazine. The new edition would come out each Monday morning.

We'd be there from sometime in the middle of the morning, and often finish at the end of the early evening rush hour, which was around 7p.m. We stayed for as long as it took us to sell a batch of papers.

Being with Bob had already taught me a lot about responsibility but the *Big Issue* took that to another level. If I wasn't responsible and organised I didn't earn money. And if I didn't earn money Bob and I didn't eat. So from that very first fortnight, I had to grasp how to run my *Big Issue* pitch as a business.

151

For someone whose life had been completely disorganised for the best part of ten years, this was a huge leap. I'd never been great with money, and had to live from hand to mouth. I surprised myself with the way I adapted to the new demands.

There were downsides, of course, there were bound to be. There is no sale or return with the *Big Issue* so I learned quickly that if you miscalculated the amount of magazines, you could lose out quite badly. You can take a serious blow if you are stuck with fifty papers on Saturday night. Come Monday, you get no credit against the next purchase from the old magazines, so the old papers are pulp. At the same time, you didn't want to under buy. Too few and you'd sell out too quickly and miss out on willing buyers. It was no different from running Marks and Spencer's — well, in theory.

The other thing you had to factor in was that there was a huge difference in the quality of the magazines from week to week. Some weeks it would be a good issue packed with interesting stuff. Other weeks it would be quite dull and really hard to sell, especially if the cover didn't have some famous film or rock star on it. It could be a bit unfair.

It took a while to get the balance right.

While I was working out the best way to sell the *Big Issue*, I still lived from hand to mouth. What I earned between Monday and Saturday evening was generally gone by Monday morning. Sometimes at the start of each week I'd turn up at the coordinator's stand with only a few quid.

If Sam was there I'd ask her to do me a favour and buy ten papers for me on the understanding I'd pay her back as soon as I had some money. She would usually do this for vendors who she knew she could trust to repay her and I had done this once or twice before when I was desperate and always repaid her within hours. I knew the money was coming out of her pocket, not the *Big Issue*'s, so it was only fair.

Then when I had sold those copies I'd go back and pay off what I owed and get some more papers. I'd build it up that way from there.

As a result of this, in real terms, I was actually making less money than I had been busking with Bob. But as I settled down into this new routine, I decided it was a price worth paying. The fact that I was working legitimately on the streets made a huge difference to me. If I got stopped by a policeman, I could produce my badge and be left in peace. After the experience with the Transport Police that meant a lot.

The next couple of months working at the tube station flew by. In many ways it was similar to busking. We'd attract the same sort of people: a lot of middle-aged and elderly ladies, groups of female students, gay guys but also people from all walks of life.

One day during the early part of the autumn of 2008 we were approached by a very flamboyant-looking guy. He had bleached-blond hair and was wearing jeans, cowboy boots and I could tell that the leather jacket and jeans must have cost a fortune. I was sure he was an American rock star; he certainly looked like one.

As he'd walked along, he had immediately spotted Bob. He stopped in his tracks and smiled.

'That's one cool cat,' he said, in a sort of transatlantic drawl.

He looked really familiar but I couldn't for the life of me place him. I was dying to ask him who he was, but thought it was rude. I was glad I didn't.

He spent a minute on his knees just stroking Bob.

'You guys been together long?' he asked.

'Uhhmm, gosh, let me think,' I said, having to work it out. 'Well we got together in the spring of last year, so it's about a year and a half now.'

'Cool. You look like real soul brothers,' he smiled. 'Like you belong together.'

'Thanks,' I said, by now desperate to know who the hell this guy was.

Before I could ask him he got up and looked at his watch.

'Hey, gotta go, see you guys around,' he said, reaching into a pocket in his jacket and producing a wad of cash.

He then dropped a tenner into my hand.

'Keep it,' he said, as I began to rummage around for change. 'You guys have a good day.'

'We will,' I promised him. And we did.

★ ★ ★

It made such a difference that I was now working outside the tube station legitimately. I'd had a couple of moments with some of the familiar

154

faces from the tube station again, one or two of whom had given me some filthy looks. I'd ignored them. The rest of the staff there were actually fine. They knew I was getting on with my job and as long as I didn't offend or harass anyone, that was fine.

Inevitably, Bob and I had also got a bit of attention from other *Big Issue* vendors in the area.

I wasn't so naive as to think that everything was going to be all sweetness and light with the other vendors and assorted street workers. Life on the streets wasn't like that. It wasn't a community built on caring for each other, it was a world in which everyone looked after number one. But, to begin with, at least, most of the other *Big Issue* sellers reacted warmly to the sight of the new guy with a cat on his shoulders.

There had always been vendors around with dogs. One or two of them had been real characters. But, as far as I was aware, there had never been a *Big Issue* seller with a cat in Covent Garden — or anywhere else in London — before.

Some of the vendors were rather sweet about it. A few of them came up and started stroking him and asking questions about how we met and what I knew about his background. The answer, of course, was nothing. He was a blank slate, a mystery cat, which seemed to endear everyone to him even more.

No one was interested in me, of course. The first thing they'd say when they saw us again was 'How's Bob today?' No one ever asked how I

155

was. But that was OK, that was to be expected. I knew the air of bonhomie wouldn't last. It never did on the streets.

★   ★   ★

With Bob at my side I discovered that I could sell as many as thirty or even fifty papers on a good day. At £2 a paper, as they were priced back then, it could add up quite well, especially with the tips that some people gave me — or, more usually, Bob.

One early autumn evening, Bob was sitting on my rucksack, soaking up the last of the day's sun, when a very well-heeled couple walked past the tube station. To judge by their outfits they were heading for the theatre or maybe even the opera. He was wearing a tuxedo and a bow tie and she had a black silk dress on.

'You two look very smart,' I said, as they stopped and started drooling over Bob.

The lady smiled at me but the guy ignored me.

'He's gorgeous,' the lady said. 'Have you been together for a long time?'

'Quite a while,' I said. 'We kind of found each other on the streets.'

'Here you go,' the guy said, suddenly pulling out his wallet and removing a twenty-pound note.

Before I could even reach into my coat to fish out some change, he'd waved me away. 'No that's fine, keep it,' he said, smiling at his companion.

The look she gave him spoke volumes. I had a feeling they were on a first date. She had clearly been impressed by him giving me that much money.

As they walked off I noticed her leaning into him and wrapping her arm into his.

I didn't care whether it was genuine or not. It was the first time I'd ever been given a twenty-pound drop.

After a few more weeks of trying out the spot at the tube station, I realised that — far from being a 'bad' pitch — the tube station was actually ideal for me and Bob. So I was disappointed when Sam told me that having finished my probation period I would be moving to another pitch at the end of the fortnight.

It wasn't exactly a surprise. The thing about being a member of the *Big Issue* vendor community is that everyone can see how well each other is doing. When the vendors go to the coordinator they can see who has been buying what quantities on a list that's there for everyone to see. You can read it and spot who has been buying papers in batches of tens and twenties and how many batches they are buying. So during that first fortnight, they would have seen that I was buying a lot of magazines.

It soon became obvious that it was something that had been spotted by some of the other vendors. In that second week I noticed a subtle but definite change in the attitude towards me.

I wasn't at all surprised when Sam told me that I'd ended my probation and would now be moved to a different pitch. Our new location wasn't a long way from the tube station, on the corner of Neal Street and Short's Gardens, outside a shoe shop called Size.

I got the distinct feeling that the older hands had taken a dislike to me and Bob and hadn't taken too kindly to us doing so well out of what was supposed to be a bad pitch. For once, however, I buttoned my lip and accepted it. *Choose your battles, James*, I counselled myself.

It turned out to be good advice.

14

Under the Weather

It was a cold and wet autumn that year. The trees were soon being stripped of their foliage as the cold winds and heavy rains began to build. On one particular morning, as Bob and I left the block of flats and set off for the bus stop, the sun was once more nowhere to be seen and a light, fine drizzle was falling.

Bob wasn't a big fan of the rain so at first I assumed it was to blame for the lethargic way in which he began padding his way along the path. He seemed to be taking each step at a time, almost walking in slow motion. *Maybe he's got second thoughts about joining me today,* I said to myself. *Or maybe it was true what they said about cats being able to sense bad weather in the air.* As I cast an eye up to the sky, a giant bank of steely, grey clouds were hovering over north London like some vast, alien spaceship. It was probably going to be like this all day. There was almost certainly some heavier rain on its way. Maybe Bob was right and we should turn around, I thought for a second. But then I remembered the weekend was coming and we didn't have enough money to get through it. *Beggars can't be choosers — even if they have been cleared of all charges,* I said to myself, trying to make light of the predicament.

I was never happy to be working on the streets of London but today it seemed an even bigger pain in the butt than usual.

Bob was still moving at a snail's pace and it had taken us a couple of minutes to get a hundred yards down the road.

'Come on, mate, climb aboard,' I said, turning around and ushering him up into his normal position.

He draped himself on my shoulder and we trudged off towards Tottenham High Road and the bus. The rain was already intensifying. Fat, heavy drops of water were bouncing off the pavement. Bob seemed fine as we sploshed our way along, ducking under any available shelter as we went. But as we settled into our bus journey I realised there was more to his low spirits than just the weather.

The ride was normally one of his favourite parts of the day. Bob was a curious cat. Normally the world was an endlessly interesting place to him. No matter how often we did it, he would never tire of pressing himself against the glass. But today he wasn't even bothered about taking the window seat — not that he'd have seen much through the condensation and streaks of rain that obscured our view of the outside world. Instead he curled up on my lap. He seemed tired. His body language was droopy. Looking at his eyes he seemed a bit drowsy, as if he was half asleep. He was definitely not his normal, alert self.

It was when we got off at Tottenham Court Road that he took a distinct turn for the worse.

Luckily the rain had eased off a bit by now and I was able to splash my way through the back-streets in the direction of Covent Garden. It wasn't an easy process and I kept hopping around to sidestep the bigger puddles and the giant umbrellas that flew at me every now and then.

As we walked down Neal Street I was suddenly aware that Bob was behaving oddly on my shoulder. Rather than sitting there impassively as normal, he was twitching and rocking around.

'You all right there, mate?' I said, slowing down.

All of a sudden he began moving in a really agitated way, making weird retching noises as if he was choking or trying to clear his throat. I was convinced he was going to jump or fall off so I placed him down on the street to see what was wrong. But before I could even kneel down he began to vomit. It was nothing solid, just bile. But it just kept coming. I could see his body convulsing as he retched and fought to expel whatever it was that was making him sick. For a moment or two I wondered whether it was my fault and he felt queasy because of all the motion today.

But then he was sick again, retching away and producing more bile. It was clearly more than motion sickness. Pretty soon he didn't have anything left to bring up, which was puzzling because he'd eaten well the night before and at breakfast. That was when I realised there must be more to it than this. He must have been sick already today, even before we left the flats, probably when he'd been in the garden doing his business. He must have been feeling sick during the bus journey too, I could now see. I blamed myself for not spotting it sooner.

It's weird how you react in a situation like that. I'm sure my instincts were the same as any parent or pet owner. All sorts of crazy, sometimes conflicting thoughts rushed through my mind. Had he simply eaten something that disagreed with him this morning? Had he swallowed something in the flat that had set him off? Or was this something more serious? Was he going to drop dead in front of me? I'd heard stories about cats collapsing in front of their owners after drinking cleaning fluids or choking on bits of plastic. For a split second, an image of Bob dying flashed through my head. I managed to pull myself together before my imagination ran riot.

Come on, James, let's deal with this sensibly, I told myself.

I knew that all the retching and the fact that he no longer had any liquid to bring up meant that he was getting dehydrated. If I didn't do anything he could do damage to one of his organs. I decided that some food and, more importantly, some water, would be a good idea. So I scraped him up and held him in my arms as we walked on to Covent Garden and a general store I knew nearby. I didn't have much cash on me at all, but I cobbled together enough to buy a liquidised chicken meal that Bob usually loved and some good, mineral water. I didn't want to risk giving him contaminated tap water. That might make matters even worse.

I carried him to Covent Garden and placed it

down on the pavement near our normal pitch. I got out Bob's bowl and spooned the chicken into it.

'Here we go, mate,' I said, stroking him as I placed the bowl in front of him.

Ordinarily he would have pounced immediately and guzzled down a bowl of food at a rate of knots, but not today. Instead he stood and looked at it for a while before he decided to tuck in. Even then he was very tentative about it, only picking at the bowl. He only ate the jelly. He didn't touch a bit of the meat. Again, it set the alarm bells ringing. This wasn't the Bob I knew and loved. Something was definitely wrong.

I half-heartedly set myself up to start selling the magazine. We needed some money to get us through the next few days, especially if I was going to have to take Bob to a vet and pay for some drugs. But my heart really wasn't in it. I was far more concerned with watching Bob than trying to capture the attention of passers-by. He lay there, impassive, uninterested in anything. Unsurprisingly, not too many people stopped to make a donation. I cut the day short after less than two hours. Bob hadn't been sick again, but he definitely wasn't right. I had to get him home to the warmth — and dryness — of the flat.

* * *

I guess I'd been lucky with Bob until now. Ever since I'd taken him under my wing, he had been in perfect health, 100 per cent tip top. He'd had fleas early on but that was to be expected of a

163

street cat. Since I'd treated him for that and given him an early worming treatment, he'd suffered no health problems at all.

Every now and again I had taken him to the Blue Cross van on Islington Green where he'd been microchipped. The vets and vet nurses there knew him well by now and always commented on what good condition he was in. So this was alien territory for me. I was terrified that it might be something serious. As he lay on my lap on the bus returning to Tottenham, I felt the emotions welling up every now and again. It was all I could do to stop myself from bursting into tears. Bob was the best thing in my life. The thought of losing him was terrifying. I couldn't keep that thought out of my head.

When we got home Bob just headed straight for the radiator where he just curled up and went straight to sleep. He stayed there for hours. That night I didn't sleep much, worrying about him. He'd been too out of it to even follow me to bed and was snoozing under the radiator in the front room. I kept hauling myself out of bed to check on him. I'd creep up in the gloom and listen for the sound of his breathing. One time I was convinced he wasn't and had to kneel down to place my hand on his diaphragm to make sure it was moving. I couldn't believe how relieved I was when I found he was purring gently.

Money was so tight I simply had to go out again the following day. That presented me with a real dilemma. Should I leave Bob in the flat on his own? Or should I wrap him up warm and take him into central London with me so that I could keep an eagle eye on him.

Luckily the weather was a lot better today. The sun had decided to make an appearance. And when I wandered out of the kitchen with my cereal bowl in my hands, I saw Bob looking up at me. He looked a little perkier today. And when I offered him a little food he nibbled at it a lot more enthusiastically.

I decided to take him with me. It was still early in the week, so I'd have to wait a few days before I could get him looked at by the Blue Cross van. So, in advance of that, I decided to do some research and headed for the local library where I logged on to a computer and started researching Bob's symptoms.

I'd forgotten what a bad idea it is to search through medical websites. They always give you the worst possible scenario.

I punched in a few key words and came across a couple of informative-looking sites. When I entered the main symptoms — lethargic, vomiting, appetite loss and a few others — a whole swathe of possible illnesses popped up.

Some weren't too bad, for instance, it could have been down to hairballs or maybe even a bad case of flatulence. But then I started looking at other possibilities. Just the As in the list were bad enough. They included Addison's disease, acute kidney disease and arsenic poisoning. As if they weren't scary enough, other options on the long list included feline leukaemia, colitis, diabetes, lead poisoning, salmonella and tonsillitis. Worst of all, as far as I was concerned, one of the sites said it could be an early sign of bowel cancer.

By the time I'd been reading for fifteen minutes or so I was a nervous wreck.

I decided to switch tack and look at the best treatments for vomiting. That was more positive. The sites I looked at suggested plenty of water, rest and supervision. So that was my plan for the next twenty-four to forty-eight hours. I'd basically keep an eye on him around the clock. If he started vomiting again, obviously, I'd head for the vet's immediately. If not, I'd go to the Blue Cross on Thursday.

★ ★ ★

The next day I decided to stay at home until late in the afternoon to give Bob a good chance to rest. He slept like a log, curled up in his favourite spot. I wanted to keep an eye on him. He seemed OK, so I decided to leave him for three or four hours and try and squeeze in some selling. I didn't have much option.

Trudging through the streets that led from Tottenham Court Road to Covent Garden I was aware of my invisibility again. When I got to Covent Garden all everyone could ask was 'Where's Bob?' When I told people that he was ill they were all really concerned. 'Is he going to be all right?'; 'Is it serious?'; 'Is he going to see a vet?'; 'Is he OK on his own at home?'

It was then that an idea struck me. I had come across a vet nurse called Rosemary. Her boyfriend, Steve, worked at a comic-book shop near where we sometimes set up. Bob and I would pop in there every now and again and we

166

had become friends. Rosemary had been in there with Steve one day and we'd struck up a conversation about Bob.

I decided to stick my head in there to see if either of them was around. Luckily Steve was there and gave me a phone number for Rosemary.

'She won't mind you ringing her,' he said. 'Especially as it's about Bob. She loves Bob.'

When I spoke to Rosemary she asked me a load of questions.

'What does he eat? Does he ever eat anything else when he's out and about?'

'Well, he rummages around in the bins,' I said.

It was a habit he had never shaken off. He was an absolute terror. I'd seen him tear the garbage bags to pieces in the kitchen. I'd have to put them outside the front door. He was a street cat. You can take the cat off the street, but you can't take the street out of the cat.

I could hear it in her voice, it was as if a light bulb had been switched on.

'Hmmm,' she said. 'That might explain it.'

She prescribed some probiotic medication, some antibiotics and some special liquid to settle the stomach.

'What's your address?' she said. 'I'll get it biked over to you.'

I was taken aback.

'Oh, I'm not sure that I can afford that, Rosemary,' I said.

'No, don't worry, it won't cost you anything. I'll just add it to another delivery in the area,' she said. 'This evening OK?'

'Yes, great,' I said.

I was overwhelmed. Such spontaneous acts of generosity hadn't exactly been a part of my life in the past few years. Random acts of violence, yes; kindness, no. It was one of the biggest changes that Bob had brought with him. Thanks to him I'd rediscovered the good side of human nature. I had begun to place my trust — and faith — in people again.

Rosemary was as good as her word. I had no doubt she would be. The bike arrived early that evening and I administered the first doses of the medicine straight away.

Bob didn't like the taste of the probiotic. He screwed his face up and recoiled half a step when I gave him his first spoonful of it.

'Tough luck, mate,' I said. 'If you didn't stick your face in rubbish bins, you wouldn't have to take this stuff.'

The medicine had an almost immediate impact. That night he slept soundly and was a lot friskier the following morning. I had to hold his head in my hand to make sure he swallowed the probiotic.

By the Thursday he was well on the road to recovery. But, just as a precaution, I decided to pop along to see the Blue Cross van on Islington Green.

The nurse on duty recognised him immediately and looked concerned when I told her Bob had been under the weather.

'Let's give him a quick check up, shall we?' she said.

She checked his weight and inside his mouth

and had a good feel around his body.

'All seems well,' she said. 'I think he's on the road to recovery.'

We chatted for a couple of minutes before I headed off.

'Just don't go rummaging in those bins any more, Bob,' the nurse said as we left the makeshift surgery.

★　★　★

Seeing Bob sick had a profound effect on me. He had seemed to be such an indestructible cat. I'd never imagined him getting ill. Discovering that he was mortal really shook me.

It underlined the feeling that had been building inside me for a while now. It was time for me to get myself clean.

I was fed up with my lifestyle. I was tired of the mind-numbing routing of having to go to the DDU unit every fortnight and the chemist every day. I was tired of feeling like I could slip back into addiction at any time.

So the next time I went to see my counsellor I asked him about coming off methadone and taking the final step towards becoming completely clean. We'd talked about it before, but I don't think he'd ever really taken me at my word. Today, he could tell I was serious.

'Won't be easy, James,' he said.

'Yeah, I know that.'

'You'll need to take a drug called Subutex. We can then slowly decrease the dosage of that so that you don't need to take anything,' he said.

'OK,' I said.

'The transition can be hard, you can have quite severe withdrawal symptoms,' he said, leaning forward.

'That's my problem,' I said. 'But I want to do it. I want to do it for myself and for Bob.'

'OK, well, I will get things moving and we will look at beginning the process in a few weeks' time.'

For the first time in years, I felt like I could see the tiniest light at the end of a very dark tunnel.

15

The Naughty List

I could sense there was something wrong the moment I arrived at the Covent Garden coordinators' stand one damp, cold Monday morning. A few other vendors were hanging around, stamping their feet to keep warm and sipping at Styrofoam cups of tea. When they noticed me and Bob, a couple of them muttered to each other and threw me dirty looks, as if I was an unwelcome guest.

When Sam, the coordinator appeared from the other side of the distribution trolley where she'd been collecting a new batch of papers, she immediately jabbed a finger at me.

'James, I need to have a word with you,' she said, looking stern.

'Sure, what's the problem?' I said, approaching her with Bob on my shoulder.

She almost always said hello to him and gave him a stroke, but not today.

'I've had a complaint. In fact, I've had a couple of complaints.'

'What about?' I said.

'A couple of vendors are saying that you are floating. You've been spotted doing it a few times around Covent Garden. You know floating is against the rules.'

'It's not true,' I said, but she just put her palm

171

up in classic 'talk to the hand' fashion.

'There's no point arguing about it. The office wants you to go in for a talk.'

I assumed that was that and headed towards the stacks of papers that had just arrived.

'Sorry, no, you can't buy any more magazines until you go into Vauxhall and sort it out.'

'What? I can't get any more magazines today?' I protested. 'How am I going to make any money for Bob and me?'

'Sorry, but you are suspended until you sort it out with head office.'

I was upset, but not entirely surprised. Things had been building up to this for a while.

One of the many rules that you have to follow as a *Big Issue* seller is that you stick to selling your papers at your designated spot. You aren't supposed to sell at someone else's pitch. And you aren't supposed to 'float', that is, to sell while you are walking around the streets. I was 100 per cent in agreement with the rule. I wouldn't have liked it if someone started walking around next to my pitch waving *Big Issues* around. It was the fairest and simplest way of policing London's army of vendors.

But during the past month or two I'd had a couple of vendors come up to me to complain that I was 'floating'. They reckoned they'd seen me selling papers while I was walking around with Bob. It wasn't true, but I could see why they might have thought it.

Walking around with Bob had always been a stop-start process. Wherever we went around London, we were stopped every few yards by people wanting to stroke him and talk to him or have a photograph taken.

The only difference now was that people would sometimes ask to buy a copy of the *Big Issue* as well.

As I explained to the other vendors, it put me in a really tricky spot. What I should technically say was, 'Sorry, you'll have to come to my pitch or buy one from the nearest vendor.' But I knew what the end result of that would be: no sale, which wouldn't benefit anyone.

A few of the vendors I'd spoken to had sympathised and understood. Quite a few others didn't, however.

I guessed immediately who had reported me. It didn't take a genius to work it out.

A month or so before Sam had issued the suspension, I'd been walking down Long Acre, past the Body Shop where a guy called Geoff had a *Big Issue* pitch. Gordon Roddick, whose wife Anita had founded the Body Shop, had strong links with the *Big Issue* so there were always vendors outside their stores. I knew him a little bit and I'd acknowledged him as I walked past. But then, a few moments later, an elderly American couple had stopped me and Bob in the street.

They were incredibly polite, your classic stereotype Midwestern husband and wife.

'Excuse me, sir,' the husband said, 'but could I just take a picture of you and your companion? Our daughter loves cats and it would make her day to see this.'

I'd been more than happy to oblige. No one

had called me 'sir' for years — if ever!

I'd got so used to posing for tourists that I'd perfected a couple of poses for Bob that seemed to work best for photographs. I would get him on my right shoulder and turn him to face forward with his face right next to mine. I did this again this morning.

The American couple was delighted with this. 'Oh, gee, I can't thank you enough. She will be thrilled to pieces with that,' the wife said.

They couldn't stop saying thank you and offered to buy a copy of the magazine. I said no and pointed to Geoff a few yards away.

'He is the official *Big Issue* vendor in this area so you should go and buy it from him,' I said.

They'd decided not to and moved on. But then just as they'd been walking off, the wife had leant towards me and squeezed a fiver into my hand.

'Here you go,' she said. 'Give yourself and your lovely cat a treat.'

It was one of those classic situations where perception and reality were the complete opposite of each other. Anyone who had been there would have seen I hadn't solicited money and had actively tried to push them towards Geoff. To Geoff, on the other hand, it looked like I'd not just taken money without handing over a magazine, something else which was forbidden, but I'd compounded the crime by telling them to ignore him.

I knew immediately that it would look bad so I headed towards him to try and explain. But I was already too late. He was shouting obscenities at me and Bob before I got within ten yards. I knew Geoff had a fiery temper and had a reputation for being punchy with it. I decided not to risk it. He was in such a rage, I didn't even try to reason with him and headed off to leave him in peace.

It was soon pretty obvious that the incident must have become, well, a big issue among the *Big Issue* vendors. After that there must have been some kind of whispering campaign against me.

It started with snide remarks.

'Floating around again today,' one vendor said to me sarcastically as I passed his pitch one morning. At least he was vaguely civil about it.

Another vendor, around St Martin's Lane, had been much more direct.

'Whose sales are you and that mangy moggie going to steal today?' he had snarled at me.

Again, I tried to explain the situation but I might as well have been talking to the wall. It was clear that vendors were gossiping to each other, putting two and two together and coming up with five.

I hadn't worried about it that much at first, but it had then escalated a little.

Not long after the incident with Geoff, I started getting threats from the drunk vendors. *Big Issue* vendors aren't supposed to drink on the job. That is one of the most fundamental rules. But the truth is that a lot of vendors are alcoholics and carry a can of extra-strength lager with them in their pockets. Others keep a flask of something stronger and take a little nip from it every now and again to keep them going. I have to hold my hands up: I'd done it myself once, on a particularly cold day. But these guys were different. They were blind drunk.

One day Bob and I were walking through the piazza when one of them lurched at us, slurring his words and waving his arms.

'You f***ing bastard, we'll f***ing get you,' he said. I wish I could say that this only happened once, but it became almost a weekly event.

The final clue that all was not well had come one afternoon when I'd been hanging around the coordinator's pitch in Covent Garden. Sam's colleague Steve would often do her afternoon shift for her.

He was always good to Bob. I don't think Steve liked me much, but he would always make a fuss of Bob. On this particular day, however, he had been in a foul mood towards us both.

I was sitting on a bench minding my own business when Steve came over to me.

'If it was up to me you wouldn't be selling,' he said, real venom in his voice. 'As far as I'm concerned you're a beggar. That's what you and that cat are doing.'

I was really upset by this. I'd come such a long way. I'd made such a huge effort to fit into the *Big Issue* family in Covent Garden. I'd explained time and again what was happening with Bob, but it made no difference. It would go in one ear and straight back out the other.

So, as I say, I wasn't entirely surprised when Sam broke the news about my having to go to head office. But it still left me reeling.

I walked away from Covent Garden dazed and not a little confused. I really didn't know what to do now that I was on the 'Naughty List'.

★ ★ ★

That night me and Bob ate our dinners then went to bed early. It was getting cold and, with the financial situation looking bleak, I didn't want to waste too much electricity. So while Bob curled up at the foot of the bed, I huddled under the covers trying desperately to work out what to do next.

I had no idea what the suspension meant. Could it mean that I would be banned for good? Or was it simply a slap on the wrists? I had no idea.

As I lay there, memories came flooding back of how my busking had been unfairly brought to an end. I couldn't bear the thought of being denied a livelihood by other people's lies a second time.

It seemed even more unfair this time. I hadn't got into any trouble until now, unlike a lot of the *Big Issue* vendors I'd seen around Covent Garden who were often breaking rules and getting told off by Sam and the other coordinators.

I knew about one guy who was notorious with all the sellers. He was this big, brash cockney geezer, a very intimidating character; he would growl at people in a really threatening voice. He'd frighten women, in particular, by going up to them and saying: 'Come on, darling, buy a magazine.' It was almost as if he was threatening them. 'Buy one, or else . . . '

Apparently he used to roll the magazine up and then slip it into people's bags as they were walking past. I'd also heard that he would then stop them and say: 'That will be two pounds, please' and then follow them until they gave him money to go away. That kind of thing doesn't help anyone. Most of the time the victims would simply toss the papers into the nearest bin. It wasn't even as if the money was going to a good cause. This brute of a man was said to be a gambling addict and other sellers said that all he did was pump it straight back into fruit machines.

He had obviously broken so many of the basic rules it was ridiculous, yet as far as I knew, he'd never been disciplined.

Whatever misdemeanours I had supposedly committed, it didn't compare to that. And it was the first time I'd been accused of anything. Surely that would count in my favour? Surely it wasn't a question of one strike and you're out? I simply didn't know. Which was why I was beginning to panic.

The more I thought about it, the more confused and helpless I felt. But I knew I couldn't just do nothing. So the following morning I decided to head out as normal and simply try another coordinator in a different part of London. It was a risk, I knew that, but I figured it was one that was worth taking.

As a *Big Issue* seller you learn that there are coordinators all over town, around Oxford

Street, King's Cross and Liverpool Street, in particular. You get to know the whole network. So I decided to chance my arm over at Oxford Street where I'd met a couple of people in the past.

I arrived at the stall mid-morning and tried to make the situation as low-key as possible. I flashed my badge and bought a pile of twenty papers. The guy there was wrapped up in other things so barely registered me. I didn't hang around long enough to give him the chance. I simply headed for a spot where there was no sign of anyone else selling and took my chances.

I felt sorry for Bob in all this. He was quite nervous and seemed disoriented, and understandably so. He liked routine, he thrived on stability and predictability. He didn't take kindly to chaos once more re-entering his life. Nor did I, to be honest. He must have been wondering why our normal routine had been so suddenly and inexplicably changed.

I managed to sell a decent number of magazines that day — and did the same the following day. I moved locations all the time, imagining that the *Big Issue* outreach team was on the lookout for me. I knew it was illogical and slightly mad, but I was paranoid, terrified that I was going to lose my job.

I had images of me being hauled in front of some committee and being stripped of my badge and cast out. 'Why is this happening to us?' I said to Bob as we headed back on the bus one evening. 'We didn't do anything wrong. Why can't we get a break?' I resigned myself to having to spend the next few weeks taking my chances in other parts of London, hoping that the coordinators didn't know I was persona non grata.

★ ★ ★

I was sitting under a battered old umbrella on a street somewhere near Victoria Station late on a Saturday afternoon when I finally told myself that I had made a mistake. Well, to be honest, it was Bob who told me.

It had been hammering down with rain for about four hours and barely a person had slowed down to stop and buy a magazine. I couldn't blame them. They just wanted to get out of the deluge.

Since we'd started selling early in the afternoon, the only people who had shown an interest in me and Bob had been the security staff of the various buildings where we'd stopped to try and take shelter.

'Sorry, mate, you can't stay here,' they'd said to me with monotonous regularity.

I'd found the umbrella discarded in a bin and had decided to use it in one last attempt to avert another mini-disaster of a day. It wasn't working.

I had been managing to get hold of papers from various vendors around London for about a month now. I had been careful about who I approached and wherever I could I got other vendors to buy papers for me. A lot of people knew who I was. But there were enough who didn't know I was on the suspended list who picked up batches of ten or twenty papers for me, to get me by. I didn't want to get them into trouble, but if they didn't know I was banned then no one could criticise them. I figured it was safe and after everything I had been through over the past few months, I just wanted to make a living and take care of myself and Bob.

It hadn't been going well though. Finding the right pitch was a real problem, mainly because most of the places I'd set up shop weren't actually licensed. Bob and I had been moved on from various street corners around Oxford Street, Paddington, King's Cross, Euston and other stations. One day, after being asked to move on three times by the same policeman, I got a semi-official warning that next time I'd be arrested. I didn't want to go through that again.

It was a real catch-22 situation. I'd made sure to steer clear of the main pitches and tried to pick places that were a bit off the beaten track. But as a result I'd found it really hard to sell the magazine, even with Bob. The *Big Issue* hadn't designated its prime sales spots by accident. They knew exactly where papers would sell — and where they wouldn't. These were the spots I'd found myself occupying.

People were still drawn to Bob, of course, but the locations just weren't right. Inevitably, this had hit me in the pocket, and it had become much harder for me to manage the business side of the *Big Issue*. Tonight I was going to hit rock bottom in that respect. I had about fifteen papers left. I knew I wasn't going to sell them and by Monday they would be out of date when a new edition came out. I was in trouble.

As the light faded and the rain continued to fall, I told myself that I'd try a couple more pitches in the hope of shifting these papers. I hadn't figured on Bob, though.

Until now he'd been as good as gold, a real stoic even on the most desperately grim day. He'd even put up with the regular splashings he got from passing cars and people, even though I knew he hated getting soaked in the cold. But when I tried to stop and sit down at the first street corner I'd spotted, he refused to stop walking. It was extremely rare that he pulled on the lead like a dog, but that's exactly what he was doing now.

'OK, Bob, I get the message, you don't want to stop there,' I said, simply thinking that he didn't fancy that particular location. But when he did exactly the same thing at the next spot and then again at the next spot after that, the penny finally dropped.

'You want to go home, don't you, Bob?' I said. He was still walking along on the lead, but on hearing this he slowed down and tilted his head almost imperceptibly in my direction, giving me what for all the world looked like a raised eyebrow. He then stopped and gave me the familiar look that said he wanted to be picked up.

In that instant I made the decision. Until now, Bob had been a rock, sticking loyally by my side despite the fact that business hadn't been so good and his bowl had consequently been a little less full of food. It just underlined to me how

182

loyal he was. Now I had to be loyal to him and get us back on track with the *Big Issue* management.

I knew it was the right thing to do. The *Big Issue* had been a great step forward for me. It had given me the biggest boost I'd had for a long time, well, since Bob had come into my life, in fact. I just needed to clear up the situation with them. I couldn't avoid facing the music any longer. For Bob's sake as much as mine. I couldn't keep doing this to him.

And so it was that the following Monday morning I had a good wash and put on a decent shirt and set off for Vauxhall. I took Bob with me, to help explain the case.

I really wasn't sure what to expect when I got there. The worst-case scenario, obviously, would be that I'd be stripped of my badge and banned from selling the magazine. That would have been grossly unfair. But I knew there would have to be some kind of punishment if they found me guilty of 'floating'. My best hope was to convince them that I hadn't been doing that.

Arriving at the *Big Issue* office I explained the situation and was told to wait.

Bob and I sat there for about twenty minutes before we got to see someone. A youngish guy and an older woman led me into a nondescript office and asked me to shut the door behind me. I held my breath and waited for the worst.

They gave me a real dressing down. They claimed I'd broken a couple of the cardinal rules.

'We've had complaints that you've been floating and begging,' they said.

I knew who had made the complaints but didn't let on. I knew I mustn't turn it into a personality clash. *Big Issue* vendors were supposed to get on with each other and if I sat there slagging off a list of other vendors it wasn't going to do me any good. Instead I tried to explain to them how difficult it was to walk around Covent Garden with Bob without being offered money for the magazine.

I gave them a couple of examples, one involving some blokes outside a pub who had stopped to admire Bob and offered me a fiver for three copies. There was an interview in there with an actress they all fancied, they told me.

'Things like that happen all the time,' I told them. 'If someone stops me outside a pub, to refuse to sell them a paper would just be rude.'

They listened sympathetically and nodded at some of the points I made.

'We can see that Bob attracts attention. We've spoken to a few vendors who have confirmed that he's a bit of a crowd puller,' the young guy said, with more than a hint of sympathy in his voice.

But when I'd finished defending myself, he leaned forward and broke the bad(ish) news. 'Well, we're still going to have to give you a verbal warning.'

'Oh, OK. A verbal warning, what does that mean?' I asked, genuinely surprised.

He explained that it wouldn't prevent me from selling, but that the situation might change if I was found guilty of floating again.

I felt a bit silly afterwards. A verbal warning

was neither here nor there. I realised that I'd panicked completely and, typically, jumped to the worst possible conclusion. I hadn't understood what was going to happen. I had been terrified that I was going to lose my job. The images I had of me being hauled in front of some committee and being stripped of my badge and cast out were just a figment of my imagination. I didn't realise it was not that serious.

I headed back to Covent Garden to see Sam, feeling slightly sheepish about what had been happening.

When she saw me and Bob, she smiled at us knowingly.

'Wasn't sure whether we'd see you two again,' she said. 'Been into the office to sort it out?'

I explained what had happened. I then gave her the piece of paper that I'd been given at the end of the meeting.

'Looks like you are back on probation for a bit,' she said. 'You can only work after 4.30p.m. and on Sundays for a few weeks. Then we can put you back on a normal shift. Just make sure to keep yourself clean. If someone comes up to you and Bob and offers to buy a magazine, say you haven't got one, or if it's obvious you have, say they are promised for regular customers. And don't get involved.'

It was all good advice, of course. The problem was that other people might want to 'get involved'. And so they did.

★   ★   ★

185

One Sunday afternoon Bob and I had headed to Covent Garden to do a couple of hours' work. Given the restrictions on us, we had to take whatever chances we could get.

We were sitting near the coordinators' spot on James Street when I was suddenly aware of a large and rather threatening presence. It was a guy called Stan.

Stan was a well-known figure in *Big Issue* circles. He'd worked for the company for years. The problem was that he was a bit unpredictable. When he was in the right frame of mind he could be the nicest guy you'd ever met. He would do anything for you, and frequently did.

He'd bailed me out and given me a couple of free papers on a couple of occasions.

However, when Stan was in a bad mood or, even worse, drunk, he could be the most objectionable, argumentative and aggressive pain in the arse in the world.

I quickly spotted that it was the latter Stan who was now standing in front of me.

Stan was a big guy, all of six feet four. He leaned down over me and bellowed: 'You aren't supposed to be here, you are banned from the area.'

I could smell his breath; it was like a distillery.

I had to stand my ground.

'No, Sam said I could come over here on Sunday or after 4.30p.m.,' I said.

Fortunately another guy who worked with Sam, Peter, was there as well and he backed me up, much to Stan's annoyance.

He lurched back for a moment then moved back in, breathing whisky fumes all over me once more. He was looking at Bob now, and not in a friendly way.

'If it was up to me I'd strangle your cat right now,' he said.

His words really freaked me out.

If he'd made a move towards Bob I would have attacked him. I would have defended him like a mother defending her child. It's the same thing. He was my baby. But I knew that would be fatal, from the *Big Issue*'s point of view. It would be the end.

So I made two decisions there and then. I picked up Bob and headed elsewhere for the afternoon. I wasn't going to work anywhere near Stan when he was in this mood. But I also made the decision to move away from Covent Garden.

It would be a wrench. Bob and I had a loyal customer base there and, besides anything else, it was a fun place to work. The inescapable truth, however, was that it was becoming an unpleasant and even a dangerous place to work. Bob and I needed to move to a less competitive part of London, somewhere where I wasn't so well known. There was one obvious candidate.

I used to busk around the Angel tube station in Islington before I went to Covent Garden. It was a good area, less lucrative than Covent Garden but still worthwhile. So I decided the next day to take a visit to the coordinator there, a great guy called Lee, who I knew a little bit.

'What are the chances of me getting a good pitch here?' I asked him.

'Well, Camden Passage is pretty busy, as is the Green, but you could do outside the tube station if you like,' he said. 'No one fancies it much.'

I had a feeling of déjà vu. It was Covent Garden all over again. For other *Big Issue* sellers in London, tube stations were reckoned to be a complete nightmare, the worst possible places to try and sell the paper. The way the theory went was that people in London are simply moving too fast, they don't have time to slow down, make the decision to buy one and dip into their pockets. They've got to be somewhere else, they are always in a hurry.

As I'd discovered at Covent Garden, however, Bob had the magical ability to slow them down. People would see him and suddenly they weren't in quite such a rush. It was as if he was providing them with a little bit of light relief, a little bit of warmth and friendliness in their otherwise frantic, impersonal lives. I'm sure a lot of people bought a *Big Issue* as a thank you for me giving them that little moment. So I was more than happy to take what was supposed to be a 'difficult' pitch right outside Angel tube.

We started that same week. I left the Covent Garden vendors to it.

Almost immediately we began to get people slowing down to say hello to Bob. We had soon picked up where we had left off in Covent Garden.

One or two people recognised us.

One evening, a well-dressed lady in a business suit stopped and did a sort of double take.

'Don't you two work in Covent Garden?' she said.

'Not any more, madam,' I said with a smile, 'not any more.'

16

Angel Hearts

The move to Angel had definitely met with Bob's seal of approval; I only had to look at his body language each day as we headed to work.

When we got off the bus at Islington Green, he wouldn't ask to climb on my shoulders in the way he tended to do when we'd been in central London. Instead, most mornings he would take the lead and march purposefully ahead of me, down Camden Passage, past all the antique stores, cafés, pubs and restaurants, and along towards the end of Islington High Street and the large paved area around the tube station entrance.

Sometimes we'd need to head to the *Big Issue* coordinator on the north side of the Green, so we'd take a different route. If that was the case, he'd always make a beeline for the enclosed garden area at the heart of the Green. I'd wait and watch while he rummaged around in the overgrowth, sniffing for rodents, birds or any other poor unsuspecting creature upon which he could test his scavenging skills. So far, he'd drawn a blank, but it didn't seem to dampen his enthusiasm for sticking his head into every nook and cranny in the area.

When we eventually arrived at his favourite spot, facing the flower stall and the newspaper stand near one of the benches by the entrance to the Angel tube station, he would stand there and watch me go through the arrival ritual, placing my bag down on the pavement and putting a copy of the *Big Issue* in front of it. Once all this was done, he would sit himself down, lick himself clean from the journey and get ready for the day.

I felt the same way about our new stamping ground. After all the trouble I'd had at Covent Garden over the years, Islington seemed like another fresh start for us both. I felt like we were starting a new era, and that this time it was going to last.

The Angel was different from Covent Garden and the streets around the West End in lots of subtle ways. In central London, the streets were mostly crammed with tourists and, in the evenings, West End revellers and theatregoers. The Angel wasn't quite as busy, but the tube station still saw a mass of humanity pouring in and out each day.

It was a distinctively different type of person, though. There were still a lot of tourists, of course, many of them drawn to the restaurants and arty venues like Sadler's Wells and the Islington Business Design Centre.

But it was also a more professional and, for want of a better word, more 'upmarket' place. Each evening I'd notice hordes of people in business suits heading in and out of the tube station. The bad news was that most of them barely even registered the fact that there was a ginger cat sitting outside the station. The good news was that a large proportion of those who did slow down and spot him took an instant shine to Bob. They were also really generous. I noticed immediately that the average purchase and tip at Islington was just that little bit bigger than in Covent Garden.

The Angel locals were also generous in a different kind of way to those in Covent Garden. Almost as soon as we began selling the *Big Issue* there, people began giving Bob bits of food.

The first time it happened was on our second or third day. A very smartly dressed lady stopped for a chat. She asked me whether we were going to be there every day from now on, which struck me as a bit suspicious. Was she going to make some sort of complaint? I was completely off the mark, however. The following day she appeared with a small Sainsbury's bag containing some cat milk and a pouch of Sheba.

'There you go, Bob,' she said happily, placing them on the pavement in front of Bob.

'He'll probably have that at home tonight if that's OK,' I said, thanking her.

'Of course,' she said. 'As long as he enjoys it that's the main thing.'

After that, more and more locals started donating titbits for him.

Our pitch was down the road from a large Sainsbury's supermarket. It soon became obvious that people were going in there to do their normal shopping and were picking up a little treat for Bob on their way round. They would then drop their presents off on their way back home.

One day, just a few weeks after we began at Angel, about half a dozen different people did this. By the end of the day, I couldn't fit all the tins of cat milk, pouches of food and tins of tuna and other fish that had been piling up all day into my rucksack. I had to keep it all in a large Sainsbury's bag. When I got back to the flat, it filled up an entire shelf in one of the kitchen cupboards. It kept us going for almost a week.

The other thing that was a world apart from Covent Garden was the attitude of the staff at the tube station. At Covent Garden I was the Antichrist, a hate figure almost. I could count the number of people with whom I'd forged a good friendship in the years I'd been busking or selling the *Big Issue* there on the fingers of one hand. In fact I didn't even need that. I could think of two at most.

By contrast, the staff at Angel were really warm and generous towards Bob from the very beginning. One day, for instance, the sun had been blazingly hot. The mercury must have been up in the 90s at one point. Everyone was walking around in shirt sleeves even though, technically, it was autumn. I was sweating like crazy in my black jeans and black T-shirt.

I deliberately placed Bob in the shade of the building behind us so that he didn't get too hot. I knew that heat was bad for cats. An hour or so after we'd set up our pitch, it became clear to me that I'd soon need to get some water for Bob. But before I was able to do something, a figure appeared from inside the tube station with a nice clean, steel bowl brimming with clear water. I recognised the lady immediately. Her name was Davika, one of the ticket attendants, she'd stopped to talk to Bob on numerous occasions already.

'Here you go, Bob,' she said, stroking him on the back of the neck as she placed the bowl in front of him. 'Don't want you getting dehydrated now, do we?' she said.

He wasted no time in diving in and lapped it up in no time whatsoever.

Bob had always had this ability to endear himself to people, but it never ceased to amaze me just how many seemed to become devoted to him. He had won the Islington crowd over in a matter of weeks. It was amazing really.

Of course, it wasn't perfect at the Angel. This was London after all. It could never have been all sweetness and light. The biggest problem was the concentration of people working the area around the tube station.

Unlike Covent Garden where all the surrounding streets were alive with activity, at the Angel things tended to be concentrated around the tube. So as a result there were a lot of other people operating on the streets, from people dishing out free magazines to charity workers — or 'chuggers', as they were known.

This was one of the biggest changes that I'd noticed since I'd started working on the streets a decade earlier. The streets were very much more competitive than they used to be. The 'chuggers' were mostly hyper-enthusiastic young people working for charities. Their job was to collar well-heeled commuters and tourists and get them to listen to a spiel about their charity. They would then try to persuade them to sign up for direct debits to be taken from their bank accounts. It was like being mugged by a charity — hence their nickname: chuggers.

Some were third world charities others were health related, to do with cancer or other illnesses like cystic fibrosis and Alzheimer's. I didn't have a problem with them being there but it was the way they hassled people that annoyed me. I had my own sales spiel for the *Big Issue*, of course. But I wasn't as intrusive or as nagging as some of these. They would follow people down the road engaging them in conversations they didn't want to have.

As a result of this, I would see people emerge from the tube station, see a wall of these enthusiastic canvassers, usually in their loud coloured T-shirts, and make a run for it. A lot of them were potential *Big Issue* buyers so it was very annoying.

If someone was really driving people away I would have a word. Some of the canvassers were fine about it. They respected me and gave me my space. But others didn't.

One day I got into a heated argument with a young student with a mop of Marc Bolan-like curls. He'd been really irritating people by bouncing around and walking alongside them as they tried to get away. I decided to have a word.

'Hey, mate, you're making life difficult for the rest of us who are working here,' I said, trying to be civil about it. 'Can you just move along the road a few yards and give us some space?'

He'd got really antsy about it. 'I've got every right to be here,' he said. 'You can't tell me what to do and I will do what I want.'

If you want to get someone's back up, you just need to say something like that. So I put him straight on the fact that while he was trying to make pocket money to fund his 'gap year', I was trying to make money to pay for my electricity and gas and to keep a roof over my and Bob's head.

His face kind of sank when I put it in those terms.

The other people who were a real irritant for me were the people who sold the assorted free magazines that were being published now. Some of them — like *StyleList* and *ShortList* — were actually good-quality magazines, so they caused me no end of problems, the simplest of which boiled down to a question: why were people going to pay for my magazine when they could get a free one from these people?

So whenever one strayed into my area I'd try to explain it to them. I'd say to them straight up: 'We all need to work, so you need to give me some space to do my job, you need to be at least twenty feet away.' It didn't always work, however, often because a lot of the vendors who sold these magazines didn't speak English. I would try to explain the situation to them but they didn't understand what I was trying to say to them. Others simply didn't want to listen to my complaints.

By far the most annoying people to work the streets around me, however, were the bucket rattlers: the charity workers who would turn up with large plastic buckets collecting for the latest cause.

Again, I sympathised with a lot of the things for which they were trying to raise money: Africa, environmental issues, animal rights. They were all great, worthwhile charities. But if the stories I had heard about how much of the money disappeared into the pockets of some of these bucket shakers were true, I didn't have much sympathy. A lot of them didn't have licences or any kind of meaningful accreditation. If you looked at the laminated badges around their necks, they could have been something from a kid's birthday party. They looked amateurish.

Yet, despite this, they were allowed inside the tube stations, a place that was an absolute no-go zone for a *Big Issue* seller. It would really nark me when I saw a bucket rattler inside the concourse hassling people. Sometimes they would be standing right up against the turnstiles. By the time they emerged out of the station the commuters and visitors were usually in no mood to be persuaded to buy the *Big Issue*.

It was, I suppose, a bit of a reversal of roles. In Covent Garden I had been the maverick who hadn't stuck to the designated areas and bent the laws a bit. Now I was on the receiving end of that.

I was the only licensed vendor in the area outside the tube station. And I'd worked out the areas that I could and couldn't stray into with the other main sellers there — the newspaper vendor and the florist in particular. The chuggers, hawkers and bucket rattlers ran roughshod over those rules. I guess some people would have thought it was ironic, but there were times when I failed to see the funny side of it, I have to admit.

17

Forty-Eight Hours

The young doctor at the DDU — the drug dependency unit — scribbled his signature at the bottom of the prescription and handed it over to me with a stern expression on his face.

'Remember, take this, then come back to me at least forty-eight hours later when you can feel the withdrawal symptoms have really kicked in,' he said, holding my gaze. 'It's going to be tough, but it will be a lot tougher if you don't stick to what I've said. OK?'

'OK, I understand,' I nodded, picking myself up and heading out of his treatment room. 'Just hope I can do it. See you in a couple of days.'

I'd been turning up at my fortnightly consultations for a couple of months since we'd first talked about coming off methadone. I thought I was ready for it, but my counsellors and doctors obviously didn't share that opinion. Each time I'd come in they had kept postponing it. I'd not got any kind of explanation as to why this was. Now, at last, they had decided it was time: I was going to make the final step towards being clean.

The prescription the counsellor had just given me was for my last dose of methadone. Methadone had helped me kick my dependence on heroin. But I'd now tapered down my usage to such an extent that it was time to stop taking it for good.

When I next came to the DDU in a couple of days' time I would be given my first dose of a much milder medication, Subutex, which would ease me out of drug dependency completely. The counsellor described the process as like landing an aeroplane, which I thought was a good analogy. In the following months he would slowly cut back my dosage until it was almost non-existent. As he did so, he said I would slowly drop back down to earth, landing — hopefully — with a very gentle bump.

As I waited for the prescription to be made up today, I didn't really dwell on the significance of it. My head was too busy with thoughts about what lay ahead during the next forty-eight hours.

The counsellor had explained the risk to me in graphic detail. Coming off methadone wasn't easy. In fact, it was really hard. I'd experience 'clucking' or 'cold turkey', a series of unpleasant physical and mental withdrawal symptoms. I had to wait for those symptoms to become quite severe before I could go back to the clinic to get my first dose of Subutex. If I didn't I risked having what's known as a precipitated withdrawal. This was basically a much worse withdrawal. It didn't bear thinking about.

I was confident at this point that I could do it. But at the same time I had an awful niggling feeling that I could fail and find myself wanting to score something that would make me feel better. But I just kept telling myself that I had to do this, I had to get over this last hurdle.

Otherwise it was going to be the same the next day and the next day and the day after that. Nothing was going to change.

This was the reality that had finally dawned on me. I'd been living this way for ten years. A lot of my life had just slipped away. I'd wasted so much time, sitting around watching the days vanish. When you are dependent on drugs, minutes become hours, hours become days. It all just slips by; time becomes inconsequential, you only start worrying about it when you need your next fix. You don't even care until then.

But that's when it becomes so awful. Then all you can think about is making money to get some more. I'd made huge progress since I'd been in the depths of my heroin addiction years earlier. The DDU had really put me back on track. But I was just sick of the whole thing now. Having to go to a chemist every day, having to visit the DDU every fortnight. Having to prove that I hadn't been using. I had had enough. I now felt like I had something to do with my life.

In a way I'd made it harder on myself by insisting on doing it alone. I had been offered the chance several times to join Narcotics Anonymous but I just didn't like the whole twelve-step programme. I couldn't do that kind of quasi-religious thing. It's almost like you have to give yourself up to a higher power. It just wasn't me.

I realised that I was making life even more difficult for myself by taking that route. The difference was I didn't think I was on my own now. I had Bob.

As usual, I didn't take him with me to the DDU clinic. I didn't like exposing him to the place. It was a part of my life I wasn't proud about, even though I did feel I'd achieved a lot since I'd first visited.

When I got home he was pleased to see me, especially as I'd stopped off at the supermarket on the way home and had a bag full of goodies intended to get us through the next two days. Anyone who is trying to get rid of an addictive habit knows what it is like. Whether it's trying to give up cigarettes or alcohol, the first forty-eight hours are the hardest. You are so used to getting your 'fix' that you can't think of anything else. The trick is to think of something else, obviously. And that's what I hoped to do. And I was just really grateful that I had Bob to help me achieve it.

That lunchtime we sat down in front of the television, had a snack together — and waited.

★   ★   ★

The methadone generally lasted for around twenty hours so the first part of the day passed easily enough. Bob and I played around a lot and went out for a short walk so that he could do his business. I played a really old version of the original *Halo 2* game on my knackered old Xbox. At that point it all seemed to be plain sailing. I knew it couldn't stay that way for much longer.

Probably the most famous recreation of someone 'clucking' is in the film *Trainspotting* in which Ewan McGregor's character, Renton, decides to rid himself of his heroin addiction. He is locked in a room with a few days of food and drink and left to get on with it. He goes through the most horrendous physical and mental experience you can imagine, getting the shakes, having hallucinations, being sick. All that stuff. Everyone remembers the bit where he imagines he is climbing inside the toilet bowl.

What I went through over the next forty-eight hours felt ten times worse than that.

The withdrawal symptoms began to kick in just after twenty-four hours after I'd had my dose of methadone. Within eight hours of that I was sweating profusely and feeling very twitchy. By now it was the middle of the night and I should have been asleep. I did nod off but I felt like I was pretty much conscious all the time. It was a strange kind of sleep, full of dreams or, more accurately, hallucinations.

It's hard to recollect exactly, but I do remember having these lucid dreams about scoring heroin. There were a lot of these dreams and they always went the same way: I would either score and spill it, score and not be able to get a needle into my vein or score but then get arrested by the police before I could use it. It was weird. It was obviously my body's way of registering the fact that it was being denied this substance that it had once been used to being fed every twelve hours or so. But it was also my subconscious trying to persuade me that maybe it was a good idea to start using it again. Deep in my brain there was obviously this huge battle of wills going on. It was almost as if I was a bystander, watching it all happen to someone else.

It was strange. Coming off heroin years ago wasn't as bad. The transition to methadone had been reasonably straightforward. This was a different experience altogether.

Time ceased to have any real meaning, but by the following morning I was beginning to experience really bad headaches, almost migraine-level pains. As a result I found it hard to cope with any light or noise. I'd try and sit in the dark, but then I'd start dreaming or hallucinating and want to snap myself out of it. It was a vicious circle.

What I needed more than anything was something to take my mind off it all, which was where Bob proved my salvation.

There were times when I wondered whether Bob and I had some kind of telepathic understanding. He could definitely read my mind sometimes, and seemed to be doing so now. He knew that I needed him so he was a constant presence, hanging around me, snuggling up close when I invited him but keeping his distance when I was having a bad time.

It was as if he knew what I was feeling. Sometimes I'd be nodding off and he would come up to me and place his face close to me, as if to say: 'You all right, mate? I'm here if you need me.' At other times he would just sit with me, purring away, rubbing his tail on me and licking my face every now and again. As I slipped in and out of a weird, hallucinatory universe, he was my sheet anchor to reality.

He was a godsend in other ways too. For a

start, he gave me something to do. I still had to feed him, which I did regularly. The process of going into the kitchen, opening up a sachet of food and mixing it in the bowl was just the sort of thing I needed to get my mind off what I was going through. I didn't feel up to going downstairs to help him do his business, but when I let him out he dashed off and was back upstairs again in what seemed like a few minutes. He didn't seem to want to leave my side.

I'd have periods where I didn't feel so bad. During the morning of the second day, for instance, I had a couple of hours where I felt much better. Bob and I just played around a lot. I did a bit of reading. It was hard but it was a way to keep my mind occupied. I read a really good non-fiction book about a Marine saving dogs in Afghanistan. It was good to think about what was going on in someone else's life.

By the afternoon and early evening of the second day, however, the withdrawal symptoms were really ramping up. The worst thing was the physical stuff. I had been warned that when you go through 'clucking' you get what's called restless legs syndrome. In effect, you have incredibly uncomfortable, nervous pulses that run through your body, making it impossible for you to sit still. I started doing this. My legs would suddenly and involuntarily start kicking — it's not called kicking the habit for nothing. I think this freaked Bob out a bit. He gave me a couple of odd, sideways looks. But he didn't desert me, he stayed there, at my side.

That night was the worst of all. I couldn't

watch television because the light and noise hurt my head. When I went into the dark, I just found my mind racing, filling up with all kinds of crazy, sometimes scary stuff. All the time my legs were kicking and I was feeling extremes of hot and cold. One minute I was so hot I felt like I was inside a furnace. The next I'd feel ice cold. The sweat that had built up all over me would suddenly start to freeze and suddenly I'd be shivering. So then I'd have to cover up and would start burning up again. It was a horrible cycle.

Every now and again, I'd have moments of lucidity and clarity. At one point I remember thinking that I really understood why so many people find it so hard to kick their drug habits. It's a physical thing as well as a mental thing. That battle of wills that's going on in your brain is very one-sided. The addictive forces are definitely stronger than those that are trying to wean you off the drugs.

At another point, I was able to see the last decade and what my addiction had done to me. I saw — and sometimes smelled — the alleys and underpasses where I'd slept rough, the hostels where I'd feared for my life, the terrible things I'd done and considered doing just to score enough to get me through the next twelve hours. I saw with unbelievable clarity just how seriously addiction screws up your life.

I had some weird, almost surreal thoughts as well. For instance, at one point it occurred to me that if I was to wake up with amnesia I'd get through the withdrawal, because I wouldn't know what was wrong with me. A lot of my problems stemmed from the fact my body knew exactly what was wrong with me and what I could do to fix it. I won't deny that there were moments of weakness when it crossed my mind, when I imagined scoring. But I was able to fend those thoughts off pretty easily. This was my chance to kick it, maybe my last chance. I had to stay strong, I had to take it: the diarrhoea, the cramps, the vomiting, the headaches, the wildly fluctuating temperatures — all of it.

★   ★   ★

That second night seemed to last forever. I'd look up at the clock and it seemed at times as if it was moving backwards. Outside it seemed as if the darkness was getting deeper and blacker rather than brightening up for morning. It was horrible.

But I had my secret weapon. Bob did annoy me at certain points. At one stage I was lying as still and quiet as possible, just trying to shut out the world. All of a sudden, I felt Bob clawing at my leg, digging into my skin quite painfully.

'Bob, what the hell are you doing?' I shouted at him a bit too aggressively, making him jump. Immediately I felt guilty.

I suspect he was worried that I was a little too still and quiet and was checking up to make sure I was alive. He was worried about me.

Eventually, a thin, soupy grey light began to seep through the window, signalling that morning had arrived at last. I hauled myself out of bed and looked at the clock. It was almost eight o'clock. I knew the clinic would be open by nine. I couldn't wait any longer.

I splashed some cold water on my face. It felt absolutely awful on my clammy skin. In the mirror I could see that I looked drawn and my hair was a sweaty mess. But I wasn't going to worry about that at this point. Instead I threw on some clothes and headed straight for the bus stop.

Getting to Camden from Tottenham at that time of the day was always a trial. Today it seemed much worse. Every traffic light was on red, every road seemed to have a long tailback of traffic. It really was the journey from hell.

As I sat on the bus, I was still having those huge temperature swings, sweating one moment, shivering the next, my limbs were still twitching every now and again, although not as badly as during the middle of the night. People were looking at me as if I was some kind of nutcase. I probably looked unbelievably bad. At that point I didn't care. I just wanted to get to the DDU.

I arrived just after nine and found the waiting room half full already. One or two people looked as rough as I felt. I wondered whether they'd been through forty-eight hours as hellish as those I'd just been through.

'Hi, James, how are you feeling,' the counsellor said as he came into the treatment room. He only needed to look at me to know the answer, of course, but I appreciated his concern.

'Not great,' I said.

'Well, you've done well to get through the last

two days. That's a huge step you've taken,' he smiled.

He checked me over and got me to give a urine sample. He then gave me a tablet of Subutex and scribbled out a new prescription, this time for some Subutex.

'That should make you feel a lot better,' he said. 'Now let's start easing you off this — and out of this place completely.'

I stayed there for a while to make sure the new medication didn't have any odd side effects. It didn't. Quite the opposite in fact, it made me feel a thousand times better.

By the time I had got back to Tottenham I felt completely transformed. It was a different feeling from what I'd experienced on methadone. The world seemed more vivid. I felt like I could see, hear and smell more clearly. Colours were brighter. Sounds were crisper. It was weird. It may sound strange, but I felt more alive again.

I stopped on the way and bought Bob a couple of new flavoured Sheba pouches that had come on to the market. I also bought him a little toy, a squeezy mouse.

Back at the flat I made a huge fuss of him.

'We did it mate,' I said. 'We did it.'

The sense of achievement was incredible. Over the next few days, the transformation in my health and life in general was huge. It was as if someone had drawn back the curtains and shed some sunlight into my life.

Of course, in a way, someone had.

18

Homeward Bound

I didn't think Bob and I could have become closer, but the experience we'd just been through together tightened our bond even more. In the days that followed, he stuck to me like a limpet, almost watching over me in case I had some kind of relapse.

There was no danger of that, however. I felt better than I had done in years. The thought of returning to the dark dependencies of the past made me shiver. I had come too far now to turn back.

I decided to celebrate my breakthrough by doing up the flat a little bit. So Bob and I put in a few extra hours each day outside the tube station and then used the proceeds to buy some paint, a few cushions and a couple of prints to put on the wall.

I then went along to a good second-hand furniture shop in Tottenham and bought a nice new sofa. It was a burgundy red, heavy-duty fabric, with a bit of luck the sort of material that would be able to resist Bob's claws. The old one was knackered, partly down to natural wear and tear, but also because of Bob's habit of scratching at its legs and base. Bob was banned from scratching the new one.

As the weeks passed and the nights turned

even darker and colder, we spent more and more time curled up on the new sofa. I was already looking forward to a nice Christmas for me and Bob, although, as it turned out, that was a little premature.

★ ★ ★

It wasn't often that I got post apart from bills, so when I saw a letter in my mailbox in the hallway of the flats one morning in early November 2008, I immediately noticed it. It was an airmail envelope and had a postmark — Tasmania, Australia.

It was from my mother.

We'd not been in proper contact for years. However, despite the distance that had formed between us, the letter was very chatty and warm. She explained that she had moved to a new house in Tasmania. She seemed to be very happy there.

The main point of her letter, however, was to offer me an invitation. 'If I was to pay your air fares to Australia and back, would you come and see me?' she asked. She explained that I could come over the Christmas holidays. She suggested I could also take in a trip to Melbourne to see my godparents, to whom I'd once been very close.

'Let me know,' she said, signing off. 'Love, Mum.'

There would have been a time when I'd have thrown the letter straight into the dustbin. I'd have been defiant and stubborn and too proud to take a handout from my family.

But I'd changed, my head was in a different place now. I had started to see life a lot more clearly and I could almost feel some of the anger and paranoia that I'd felt in the past falling away. So I decided to give it some thought.

It wasn't a straightforward decision, far from it. There were lots of pros and cons to take into consideration.

The biggest pro, obviously, was that I'd get to see my mother again. No matter what ups and downs we'd had over the years, she was my mother and I missed her.

We'd been in contact a couple of times since I'd fallen through the cracks and ended up on the streets but I'd never been honest with her about what had really happened. We'd met once in the past ten years, when she'd come to England briefly. I'd gone to meet her in a pub near Epping Forest. I'd taken the District Line up there and spent three or four hours with her. When I'd not returned as expected after six months, I'd spun her a story about having formed a band in London and said I wasn't going to come back to Australia while we were 'trying to make it big'.

I stuck to that story when I met her in the pub.

I hadn't felt great about telling her a pack of lies, but I didn't have the courage or the strength to tell her that I was sleeping rough, hooked on heroin and basically wasting my life away.

I had no idea whether she believed me or not. At that point in my life, I really didn't care.

We'd talked occasionally after that, but frequently I would go for months on end without making contact, which had obviously caused her a lot of grief.

She'd gone to amazing lengths to get hold of me at times. I hadn't thought to ring her when the 7/7 bombings happened in London in July 2005, I was — thankfully — nowhere near the blasts, but — stuck on the other side of the world — my mother had no idea that I was all right. Nick, whom she was still with, was serving in the police force in Tasmania at the time. Somehow he managed to persuade a member of the Met to do him and my mum a favour. They looked me up on their records and sent a couple of cops round to my B&B in Dalston one morning.

They scared the living daylights out of me when they arrived banging on the doors.

'Don't worry mate, you haven't done anything wrong,' one of them said when I opened the door, looking petrified probably. 'There are just a couple of people on the other side of the world who want to know you are alive.'

I had been tempted to make a joke and say that they'd almost given me a heart attack but I decided against it. They didn't look like they were that pleased to have been given the job of checking up on me.

I contacted Mum and reassured her that I was OK. Again, I hadn't even considered that somebody else might have been concerned about me. I didn't think that way at that time. I was on my own and concerned only with my own survival. But now I'd changed.

After all the years of neglect and deception, it would be a chance to make it up to her and to put the record straight. I felt like I needed to do that.

The other obvious positive was that I'd get to have a decent holiday in the sun, something that I had been deprived of for years living in London and working mostly in the evenings. I still felt drained by the experience of switching to my new medication and knew that a few weeks in a nice environment would do me the power of good. My mother told me she was living on a little farm way out in the middle of nowhere, near a river. It sounded idyllic. Australia, or more specifically, the Australian landscape, had always occupied a special place in my heart. Reconnecting with it would be good for my soul.

The list of pros were long. The list of cons, however, was even longer. And at the top of the list was my biggest concern of all: Bob. Who would look after him? How could I be sure he'd be there waiting for me when I got back? Did I actually want to be separated from my soulmate for weeks on end?

The answer to the first question presented itself almost immediately.

The moment I mentioned it Belle volunteered to look after him at her flat. I knew she was totally trustworthy and would take care of him. But I still wondered what the effect would be on him.

The other big concern was money. My mother might have been offering to pay for my fare, but

213

I still wouldn't be allowed into Australia without any money. I did some digging around and found that I'd need at least £500 in cash to gain admittance.

I spent a few days weighing up both sides of the argument but eventually decided I'd go. Why not? A change of scenery and some sunshine would do me good.

I had a lot to do. For a start I had to get a new passport, which wasn't easy given the way my life had disintegrated in recent years. A social worker gave me a hand and helped me organise the necessary paperwork, including a birth certificate.

I then had to sort out the flights. The best deal by far was to fly with Air China to Beijing and then down to Melbourne. It was a much longer journey and involved a lengthy stop-off in Beijing. But it was way cheaper than anything else on the market. My mother had given me an email address by now. I sent her an email with all the details, including my new passport number. A few days later I got a confirmation email from the website through which my mother had booked the tickets. I was on my way.

All I had to do now was raise £500. Easy.

The flight I'd found was heading to Australia in the first week of December. So for the next few weeks, I worked every hour of the day in all weather. Bob came with me most days, although I left him at home when it was raining heavily. I knew he didn't like it and I didn't want to risk him catching a chill or getting ill before I went away. There was no way I'd be able to go to

Australia knowing he was ill again.

I was soon saving up a bit of cash, which I kept in a little tea caddy I'd found. Slowly but surely it began to fill up. As my departure date loomed into view, I had enough to make the trip.

★ ★ ★

I headed to Heathrow with a heavy heart. I'd said goodbye to Bob at Belle's flat. He'd not looked too concerned, but then he had no idea I was going to be away for the best part of six weeks. I knew he'd be safe with Belle but it still didn't stop me fretting. I really had become a paranoid parent.

If I'd imagined the trip to Australia was going to be a nice, relaxing adventure I was sorely mistaken. The thirty-six hours or so it took me was an absolute nightmare.

It started quietly enough. The Air China flight to Beijing took eleven hours and was uneventful. I watched the in-flight movie and had a meal but I found it hard to sleep because I wasn't feeling fantastic. It was partly because of my medication but partly also because of the damp London weather. Maybe I'd spent too many hours selling the *Big Issue* in the pouring rain. I had a horrendous cold and kept sneezing all the way through the flight. I got a few funny looks from the air stewardesses and some of my fellow passengers when I had a bad attack, but thought nothing of it until we landed in Beijing.

As we taxied towards the terminal, there was an announcement from the captain over the tannoy. It was in Chinese first but there was then an English translation. It basically said that we should stay in our seats until we were asked to leave the plane.

'Odd,' I thought.

The next thing I saw was two uniformed Chinese officials wearing facemasks. They were walking down the aisle — straight towards me. When they got to me, one of them produced a thermometer.

An air stewardess was standing there to translate. 'These men are from the Chinese government. They need to take your temperature,' she said.

'OK,' I said, sensing this wasn't the time to argue.

I opened wide and sat there while one of the officials kept looking at his watch. After they'd muttered something in Chinese the air hostess said: 'You need to go with these men to undergo some routine medical checks.'

It was 2008 and we were at the height of the swine flu scare. China, in particular, was being incredibly nervous about it. I'd watched a report on the news a few days earlier in which they'd talked about the way people were being turned away from China if there was the slightest hint of them being infected. A lot of people were being placed in quarantine and held there for days.

So I was a bit apprehensive as I walked off with them. I had visions of me being holed up in some Chinese isolation ward for a month.

They ran all sorts of tests on me, from blood tests to swabs. They probably found all sorts of interesting things — but they found no trace

216

of swine flu, SARS or anything else contagious. After a couple of hours, a mildly apologetic official told me that I was free to go.

The only problem was that I now had to make my way back to my connecting flight and I was lost inside the humongous, hangar-like space that is Beijing airport.

I had about three hours to find my luggage and my connecting flight. It had been years since I'd spent any time in an airport terminal. I'd forgotten how big and soulless they were, and this one was especially so. I had to take a train from one part of Terminal 3 to another part.

After a few wrong turns I found my connecting flight less than an hour before it was due to take off.

I breathed a huge sigh of relief when I sank into my seat on the plane and slept like a log on the flight to Melbourne, mainly through exhaustion. But then at Melbourne I hit another snag.

As I made my way through the customs area I was suddenly aware of a Labrador dog sniffing animatedly at my luggage.

'Excuse me, sir, would you mind coming this way with us,' a customs guard said.

'Oh God,' I thought. 'I'm never going to get to meet my mother.'

I was taken to an inspection room where they started going through my stuff. They then ran an electric drug detector over my bag. I could tell there was a problem from the expressions on their faces.

'I'm afraid your luggage has tested positive for cocaine,' the guard said.

I was gobsmacked. I had no idea how that was possible. I didn't take cocaine and didn't really know anyone who did. None of my friends could afford it.

As it turned out, they said that it wasn't illegal for me to have traces of it for private use.

'If you are a casual user and it's for private consumption all you have to do is tell us and you can be on your way,' the guard said.

I explained my situation. 'I'm on a drug recovery programme so I don't take anything casually,' I said. I then showed them a letter I had from my doctor explaining why I was on Subutex.

Eventually they had to relent. They gave me a final pat down and released me. By the time I emerged from the customs area, almost an hour had passed. I had to get another flight down to Tasmania, which took another few hours. By the time I got there, it was early evening and I was utterly exhausted.

★　★　★

Seeing my mother was wonderful. She was waiting at the airport in Tasmania and gave me a couple of really long hugs. She was crying. She was pleased to see me alive, I think.

I was really happy to see her too although I didn't cry.

The cottage was every bit as lovely as she'd described it in her letter. It was a big, airy bungalow with huge garden space at the back. It was surrounded by farmland with a river running by the bottom of her land. It was a very peaceful, picturesque place. Over the next month I just hung out there, relaxing, recovering and rebooting myself.

Within a couple of weeks I felt like a different person. The anxieties of London were — literally — thousands of miles away, just over ten thousand, to be precise. My mum's maternal instincts kicked in and she made sure I was fed well. I could feel my strength returning. I could also sense me and my mother were repairing our relationship.

At first we didn't talk in great depth about things, but in time I began to open up. Then one night as we sat on the veranda, watching the sun go down, I had a couple of drinks and suddenly it all came out. It wasn't a big confession, there was no Hollywood drama. I just talked . . . and talked.

The emotional floodgates had been waiting to burst open for a while now. For years I had used drugs to escape from my emotions, in fact to make sure I didn't have any. Slowly but surely I'd changed that. And now my emotions were coming back.

As I explained some of the lows I'd been through over the last ten years, my mother looked horrified, as any parent would have done.

'I guessed you weren't doing so great when I saw you, but I never guessed it was that bad,' she said, close to tears.

At times she just sat there with her head in her hands muttering the word 'why' every now and again.

'Why didn't you tell me you'd lost your passport?'

'Why didn't you call me and ask for help?'

'Why didn't you contact your father?'

Inevitably, she blamed herself for it. She said she felt like she'd let me down, but I told her I didn't blame her. The reality was that I had let myself down. Ultimately, there was no one else to blame.

'You didn't decide to sleep in cardboard boxes and get off your face on smack every night. I did,' I said at one point. That set her off crying as well.

Once we'd broken the ice, so to speak, we talked much more easily. We talked a little about the past and my childhood in Australia and England. I felt comfortable being honest with her. I said that I'd felt she'd been a distant figure when I'd been younger and that being raised by nannies and moving around a lot had had an impact on me.

Naturally that upset her, but she argued that she'd been trying to provide an income for us, to keep a roof over our heads. I took her point, but I still wished she'd been there more for me.

We laughed a lot too; it wasn't all dark conversation. We admitted how similar we were and chuckled at some of the arguments we used to have when I was a teenager.

She admitted that there had been a big conflict of personality there.

'I'm a strong personality and so are you. That's where you get it from,' she said.

But we spent most of the time talking about

the present rather than the past. She asked me all sorts of questions about the rehab process I'd been through and what I was hoping to achieve now that I was almost clean. I explained that it was still a case of taking one step at a time, but that, with luck, I'd be totally clean within a year or so. Sometimes she just simply listened, which was something she hadn't always done. And so did I. I think we both learned a lot more about each other, not least the fact that deep down we were very similar, which is why we clashed so much when I was younger.

During those long chats, I often talked about Bob. I'd brought a photo of him with me, which I showed everyone and anyone who took an interest.

'He looks a smart cookie,' my mother smiled when she saw it.

'Oh, he is,' I said, beaming with pride. 'I don't know where I'd been now if it wasn't for Bob.'

Spending time in Australia was great. It allowed me to clear my mind. It also allowed me to take stock of where I was — and where I wanted to go from here.

There was a part of me that hankered to move back. I had family here. There was more of a support network than I had in London, certainly. But I kept thinking about Bob and the fact that he'd be as lost without me as I'd be without him. I didn't take the idea seriously for very long. By the time I'd started my sixth week in Australia, I was mentally already on the plane back to England.

I said goodbye to my mother properly this time. She came to the airport with me and waved me off on my way to Melbourne, where I was going to spend some time with my godparents. They had been quite significant figures in my youth. They had owned what was then the biggest private telecom company in Australia and were the first to form a radio pager company in the country so had a lot of money at one point. As a boy, naturally, I used to love spending time at the mansion they'd built in Melbourne. I even lived with them for a while when me and my mother weren't getting on very well.

Their reaction to my story was the same as my mother's — they were shocked.

They offered to help me out financially and even to find me work in Australia. But again I had to explain that I had responsibilities back in London.

★ ★ ★

The journey back was much less eventful than the outward trip. I felt much better, fitter and healthier and probably looked it so I didn't attract so much attention at customs or immigration control. I was so rested and revived by my time in Australia that I slept for most of the trip.

I was dying to see Bob again, although a part of me was concerned that he might have changed or even forgotten me. I needn't have had any concerns.

The minute I walked into Belle's flat his tail popped up and he bounced off her sofa and ran up to me. I'd brought him back a few little presents, a couple of stuffed kangaroo toys. He was soon clawing away at one of them. As we headed home that evening, he immediately scampered up my arm and on to my shoulders as usual. In an instant the emotional and physical journey I'd made to the other side of the world was forgotten. It was me and Bob against the world once more. It was as if I'd never been away.

19

The Stationmaster

Australia had been great, it had given me a boost both physically and emotionally. Back in London, I felt stronger and more sure of myself than I'd felt in years. Being reunited with Bob had lifted my spirits even more. Without him, a little part of me had been missing down in Tasmania. Now I felt whole again.

We were soon back into the old routine, sharing every aspect of our day-to-day life. Even now, after almost two years together, he remained a constant source of surprise to me.

I'd talked endlessly about Bob while I was away, telling everyone how smart he was. There had been times, I'm sure, when people looked at me as if I was crazy. 'A cat can't be that smart,' I'm sure they were thinking. A couple of weeks after I got back, however, I realised that I'd been underselling him.

Doing his business had always been a bit of a chore for Bob. He'd never taken to the litter trays that I'd bought him. I still had a few packs of them in the cupboard gathering dust. They'd been there since day one.

It was a real palaver having to go all the way down five flights of stairs and out into the grounds to do his business every single time he needed to go to the loo. I'd noticed in the past

224

few months, before I'd gone to Australia and again now that I was back, that he wasn't going to the toilet downstairs so often any more.

For a while I'd wondered whether it might be a medical problem and I'd taken him to the Blue Cross truck on Islington Green to have him checked out. The vets found nothing untoward and suggested that it might just be a change in his metabolism as he got older.

The explanation was actually far less scientific — and a lot more funny — than that. One morning, soon after I'd got back from Australia, I woke up really early, around 6.30a.m. My body clock was still all over the place. I hauled myself out of bed and stepped, bleary-eyed towards the toilet. The door was half open and I could hear a light, tinkling sort of noise. *Weird*, I thought. I half expected to find someone had sneaked into the flat to use the toilet, but when I gently nudged open the door I was greeted by a sight that left me totally speechless: Bob was squatting on the toilet seat.

It was just like that scene in the movie *Meet the Parents* when Robert De Niro's cat, Mr Jinxie, does the same thing. Except in this case, it was absolutely real. Bob had obviously decided that going to the toilet downstairs was too much of a hassle. So, having seen me go to the toilet a few times in the past three years, he'd worked out what he needed to do and simply mimicked me.

When he saw me staring at him, Bob just fired me one of his withering looks, as if to say: 'What are you looking at? I'm only going to the loo,

225

what could be more normal than that?' He was right of course. Why was I surprised at anything Bob did? He was capable of anything, surely I knew that already.

★ ★ ★

Our absence for a few weeks had definitely been noticed by a lot of the locals at the Angel. During our first week back on the pitch a succession of people came up to us with big smiles. They'd say things like: 'Ah, you're back' or 'I thought you'd won the lottery.' They were almost all genuine, warm-hearted welcomes.

One lady dropped off a card with 'We Missed You' written on it. It felt great to be 'home'.

As ever, of course, there were also one or two who weren't so pleased to see us.

One evening I found myself getting into a very heated argument with a Chinese lady. I'd noticed her before, looking rather disapprovingly at me and Bob. This time she approached me, waving her finger at me as she did so.

'This not right, this not right,' she said angrily.

'Sorry, what's not right?' I said, genuinely baffled.

'This not normal for cat to be like this,' she went on. 'Him too quiet, you drug him. You drug cat.'

That was the point at which I had to take issue with her.

It was far from the first time that someone had insinuated this. Back in Covent Garden when we'd been busking, a very snotty, professorial guy had stopped one day and told me in no uncertain terms that he was 'on to me'.

'I know what you're doing. And I think I know what you're giving him to stay so docile and obedient,' he said, a bit too pleased with himself.

'And what would that be then, sir?' I said.

'Ah, that would give you the advantage and you would be able to change to something else,' he said, a bit taken aback that I was challenging him.

'No, come on, you've made an accusation, now back it up,' I said stepping up my defence.

He had disappeared into thin air fairly quickly, probably quite wisely because I think I might have planted one on him if he'd carried on like that.

The Chinese woman was basically making the same accusation. So I gave her the same defence.

'What do you think I am giving him that makes him like that?' I said.

'I don't know,' she said. 'But you giving him something.'

'Well, if I was drugging him, why would he hang around with me every day? Why wouldn't he try and make a run for it when he got the chance? I can't drug him in front of everyone.'

'Psssh,' she said, waving her arms at me dismissively and turning on her heels. 'It not right, it not right,' she said once more as she melted into the crowd.

This was a reality that I'd accepted a long time ago. I knew there were always going to be some people who were suspicious that I was mistreating Bob, didn't like cats or simply didn't like the fact a *Big Issue* seller had a cat rather than a dog, which was far more common. A couple of weeks after the row with the Chinese lady, I had another confrontation, a very different one this time.

Since the early days in Covent Garden, I'd regularly been offered money for Bob. Every now and again someone would come up to me and ask 'How much for your cat?' I'd usually tell them to go forth and multiply.

Up here at the Angel I'd heard it again, from one lady in particular. She had been to see me several times, each time chatting away before getting to the point of her visit.

'Look, James,' she would say. 'I don't think Bob should be out on the streets, I think he should be in a nice, warm home living a better life.'

Each time she'd end the conversation with a question along the lines of: 'So how much do you want for him?'

I'd rebuff her each time, at which point she'd start throwing figures at me. She'd started at one hundred pounds, then gone up to five hundred.

Most recently she'd come up to me one evening and said: 'I'll give you a thousand pounds for him.'

I'd just looked at her and said: 'Do you have children?'

'Erm, yes, as a matter of fact I do,' she spluttered, a bit thrown.

'You do, OK. How much for your youngest child?'

'What are you talking about?'

'How much for your youngest child?'

'I hardly think that's got anything to do — '

I cut her off. 'Actually, I think it does have a lot to do with it. As far as I'm concerned Bob is my child, he's my baby. And for you to ask me whether I'd sell him is *exactly* the same as me asking you how much you want for your youngest child.'

She'd just stormed off. I never saw her again.

The attitude of the tube station staff was the complete polar opposite of this. One day I was talking to one of the ticket inspectors, Vanika. She loved Bob and was chuckling at the way countless people were stopping and talking to him and taking his picture.

'He's putting Angel tube station on the map, isn't he?' she laughed.

'He is, you should put him on the staff, like that cat in Japan who is a stationmaster. He even wears a hat,' I said.

'I'm not sure we've got any vacancies,' she giggled.

'Well, you should at least give him an ID card or something,' I joked.

She looked at me with a thoughtful look on her face and went away. I thought nothing more about it.

A couple of weeks later Bob and I were sitting outside the station one evening when Vanika appeared again. She had a big grin on her face. I was immediately suspicious.

'What's up?' I said.

'Nothing, I just wanted to give Bob this,' she smiled. She then produced a laminated travel card with Bob's photograph on it.

'That's fantastic,' I said.

'I got the picture off the Internet,' she said to my slight amazement. What the hell was Bob doing on the Internet?

'So what does it actually mean?' I said.

'It means that he can travel as a passenger for free on the underground,' she laughed.

'I thought that cats went free anyway?' I smiled.

'Well, it actually means we are all very fond of him. We think of him as part of the family.'

It took a lot of willpower to stop myself from bursting into tears.

20

The Longest Night

The spring of 2009 should have been on its way, but the evenings remained dark and dismal. By the time I finished selling the *Big Issue* at Angel around seven o'clock most evenings, dusk was already descending and the streetlights were blazing into life, as were the pavements.

After being quiet during the early months of the year when there were fewer tourists around, the Angel had suddenly come alive. The early evening rush hour was as busy as I'd ever seen it with what seemed like hundreds of thousands of people pouring in and out of the tube station.

Maybe it was the well-heeled crowds. The change had attracted other people to the area as well — unfortunately.

Living on the streets of London gives you really well-developed radar when it comes to sussing out people whom you want to avoid at all costs. It was around 6.30 or 7p.m., during the busiest part of the day for me, when a guy who had set off that radar a few times loomed into view.

I'd seen him once or twice before, luckily from a distance. He was a really rough-looking character. I know I wasn't exactly the most well-groomed guy on the streets of London, but this guy was really scraggy. He looked like he was sleeping rough. His skin was all red and blotchy and his clothes were smeared in dirt. What really stuck out about him, however, was his dog, a giant Rottweiler. It was black with brown markings and from the moment I first saw it I could tell immediately that it was aggressive. The sight of them walking around together reminded me of an old drawing of Bill Sikes and his dog Bull's Eye in *Oliver Twist*. You could tell they were never far away from trouble.

The dog was with him this evening as he arrived near the tube station entrance and sat down to talk to some other shifty-looking characters, who had been sitting there drinking lager for an hour or more. I didn't like the look of them at all.

Almost immediately I could see that the Rottweiler had spotted Bob and was straining at the lead, dying to come and have a go at him. The guy seemed to have the big dog under control, but it was by no means certain that it would stay that way. He seemed more interested in talking to these other guys — and getting stuck into their lager.

As it happened, I was in the process of packing up for the evening in any case. The gang's arrival only cemented that decision in my mind. I had a bad feeling about them — and the dog. I wanted to get myself and Bob as far away from them as possible.

I began gathering up my *Big Issues* and placing my other bits and pieces in my rucksack. All of a sudden I heard this really loud, piercing bark. What happened next seemed like it was in slow motion, a bad action scene from a bad action movie.

I turned round to see a flash of black and brown heading towards me and Bob. The guy had obviously not tethered the lead correctly. The Rottweiler was on the loose. My first instinctive reaction was to protect Bob, so I just jumped in front of the dog. Before I knew it he'd run into me, bowling me over. As I fell I managed to wrap my arms around the dog and we ended up on the floor, wrestling. I was shouting and swearing, trying to get a good grip on its head so that it couldn't bite me, but the dog was simply too strong.

Rottweilers are powerful dogs and I have no doubt that if the fight had gone on a few seconds longer, I'd have come off second best. God only knows what sorts of wounds it would have inflicted. Fortunately I was suddenly aware of another voice shouting and I felt the power of the dog waning as it was pulled in another direction.

'Come here, you f*****,' the owner was shouting, pulling as hard as he could on the lead. He then walloped the dog across the head with something blunt. I don't know what it was but the sound was sickening. In different circumstances I'd have been worried for the dog's welfare, but my main priority was Bob. He must have been terrified by what had just happened. I turned to check on him but found the spot where he'd been sitting empty. I spun around 360 degrees to see if someone had perhaps picked him up to protect him but there was no sign of him. He'd disappeared.

Suddenly, I realised what I'd done. I had a pile of *Big Issues* a short distance away from our pitch, under a bench. Bob's lead didn't extend that far, so, in my anxiety to get away from the Rottweiler and his owner, I had unclipped the lead from my belt. It had only been for a second or two while I gathered everything together, but that had been long enough. That was my big mistake. The Rottweiler must have been watching it all, and Bob, and must have spotted this. That's why he'd broken free and charged at us at that precise moment.

I was immediately thrown into a blind panic.

A few people had gathered around to ask me if I was OK.

'I'm fine. Anyone seen Bob?' I said, even though I wasn't actually fine. I'd hurt myself when the Rottweiler had knocked me over and I had cuts to my hands where he'd bitten me. At that moment a regular customer of mine appeared, a middle-aged lady who often gave Bob treats. She had clearly seen the commotion and came over.

'I just saw Bob, running off in the direction of Camden Passage,' she said. 'I tried to grab his lead but he was too quick.'

'Thanks,' I said, as I just grabbed my rucksack and ran, my chest pounding.

My mind immediately flashed back to the time he'd run off in Piccadilly Circus. For some reason though, this felt like a more serious situation. Back then he had basically been spooked by a man in a funny outfit. This time he'd been in real physical danger. If I hadn't intervened the Rottweiler would almost certainly have attacked him. Who knows what impact the sight of the charging dog had had on him? Perhaps it was a reminder of something he'd seen in his past? I had no idea what he must be feeling, although I guessed he was as frightened and distressed as me.

I ran straight towards Camden Passage, dodging the early evening crowds milling around the pubs, bars and restaurants.

'Bob, Bob,' I kept calling, drawing looks from passers-by. 'Anyone seen a ginger tom running this way with his lead trailing after him?' I asked a group of people standing outside the main pub in the passage.

They all just shrugged their shoulders.

I had hoped that, just as he had done that time back in Piccadilly Circus, Bob would find refuge in a shop. But by now most of them were shuttered up for the evening. It was only the bars, restaurants and cafés that were open. As I made my way down the narrow lane and asked around, I was greeted by nothing but shakes of the head. If he'd gone beyond Camden Passage heading north, then he would have ended up on Essex Road, the main road leading to Dalston and beyond. He'd walked part of that route before but never at night or on his own.

I was beginning to despair when I met a woman towards the end of the Passage, a short distance before it opens out opposite Islington Green. She pointed down the road.

'I saw a cat running down the road that way,'

she said. 'It was going like a rocket, it didn't look like it was going to stop. It was veering towards the main road, it looked like it was thinking about crossing.'

At the end of the passage, I emerged out on to the open street and scanned the area. Bob was fond of Islington Green and often stopped to do his business there. It was also where the Blue Cross vans would park. It was worth a look. I quickly crossed the road and ran into the small, enclosed grassy area. There were some bushes there where he often rummaged around. I knelt down and looked inside. Even though the light had gone and I was barely able to see my hand in front of me, I hoped against hope that I might see a pair of bright eyes staring back at me.

'Bob, Bob, are you here mate?' But there was nothing.

I walked down to the other corner of the enclosed Green and shouted a couple more times. But, apart from groans from a couple of drunks who were sitting on one of the benches, all I could hear was the insistent droning of the traffic.

I left the Green and found myself facing the big Waterstone's bookshop. Bob and I often popped in there and the staff there always made a fuss of him. I knew I really was clutching at straws now, but maybe he had headed there for refuge.

It was quiet inside the store and some of the staff were getting ready to shut up for the evening. There were just a few people browsing the shelves.

I recognised one of the ladies behind the till.

By now I was sweating, breathing heavily and must obviously have looked agitated.

'Are you all right?' she asked.

'I've lost Bob. A dog attacked us and Bob ran off. He didn't come in here did he?'

'Oh, no,' she said, looking genuinely concerned. 'I've been here and I've not seen him. But let me ask upstairs.'

She picked up the phone and dialled to the other department.

'You haven't seen a cat up there have you?' she said. The slow, shake of her head that followed told me all I needed to know. 'I'm really sorry,' she said. 'But if we do see him we'll make sure to keep him.'

'Thanks,' I said.

It was only then, as I wandered back out of Waterstone's and into the now dark evening, that it hit me. I've lost him.

I was in bits. For the next few minutes I was in a daze. I carried on walking down Essex Road, but by now I had given up on asking in the cafés, restaurants and pubs.

This was the route we came in every day — and went home again every night. When I saw a bus bound for Tottenham, another thought formed in my frazzled mind. He couldn't have? Could he?

There was an inspector standing at one of the bus stops and I asked him whether he'd seen a cat getting on a bus. I knew Bob, he was smart enough to do it. But the guy just looked at me like I'd asked him whether he'd seen aliens getting on the number 73. He just shook his head and turned away from me.

I knew cats had a great sense of direction and have been known to make long journeys. But there was no way he was going to find his way all the way back to Tottenham. It was a good three and a half miles, through some pretty rough parts of London. We'd never walked that way, we'd only ever done it on the bus. I quickly decided that was simply a non-starter.

The next half hour or so was a rollercoaster of conflicting emotions. One minute I'd convince myself that he couldn't stray far without being found and identified. Loads of people locally knew who he was. And even if he was found by someone who didn't know him, if they were sensible they would see that he was micro-chipped and would know that all his data was at the national microchip centre.

No sooner had I reassured myself of that, than a stream of very different consciousness began washing over me as, all of a sudden, a nightmare series of thoughts started pinging away in my head.

This might have been what happened three years ago. This might have been how he'd come to end up in my block of flats that spring evening. This might have been the trigger for him to decide it was time to move on again. Inside I was utterly torn. The logical, sensible side of me was saying, 'He will be OK, you'll get him back.' But the wilder, more irrational side of me was saying something much bleaker. It was saying: 'He's gone, you won't see him again.' I wandered up and down Essex Road for the best part of an

238

hour. It was now pitch dark, and the traffic was snarled up virtually all the way back to the end of Islington High Street. I was all at sea. I really didn't know what to do. Without really thinking, I just started walking down Essex Road towards Dalston. My friend Belle lived in a flat about a mile away. I'd head there.

I was walking past an alleyway when I saw a flash of a tail. It was black and thin, very different to Bob's, but I was in such a state my mind was playing tricks and I convinced myself it must be him.

'Bob,' I shouted, diving into the dark space, but there was nothing there.

Somewhere in the dark I heard a meowing sound. It didn't sound like him. After a couple of minutes, I moved on.

By now the traffic had eased off. The night suddenly fell ominously quiet. For the first time I noticed that the stars were out. It wasn't quite the Australian night sky but it was still impressive. A few weeks ago I'd been staring at the stars in Tasmania. I'd told everyone in Australia that I was coming back to care for Bob. *A fine job I've done of that*, I said, inwardly cursing myself.

For a moment or two I wondered whether my extended stay in Australia had actually been a factor in all this. Had that time apart loosened the ties between me and Bob? Had the fact that I'd been absent for six weeks made him question my commitment to him? When the Rottweiler had attacked, had he decided that he could no longer rely on me to protect him? The thought made me want to scream.

As Belle's road loomed into view I was still feeling close to tears. What was I going to do without him? I'd never find a companion like Bob again. It was then that it happened. For the first time in years I experienced an overwhelming need for a fix.

I tried to bat it away immediately, but once more my subconscious started fighting a battle of wills. Somewhere inside my head I could feel myself thinking that if I really had lost Bob, I wouldn't be able to cope, I'd have to anaesthetise myself from the grief I was already feeling.

Belle had, like me, been fighting for years. But I knew her flatmate still dabbled. The closer I got to her street, the more terrifying the thoughts in my head were becoming.

By the time I reached Belle's house, it was approaching ten o'clock. I had been wandering the streets for a couple of hours. In the distance, the sirens were wailing once more, the cops were on their way to another stabbing or punch-up in a pub. I couldn't have cared less.

As I walked up the path to the dimly lit front entrance I spotted a shape sitting quietly in the shadows to the side of the building. It was unmistakably the silhouette of a cat, but I'd given up hope by now and just assumed it was another stray, sheltering from the cold. But then I saw his face, that unmistakeable face.

'Bob.'

He let out a plaintive meow, just like the one in the hallway three years ago, as if to say: 'Where have you been? I've been waiting here for ages.'

I scooped him up and held him close.

'You are going to be the death of me if you keep running away like that,' I said, my mind scrambling to work out how he'd got here.

It wasn't long before it all fell into place. I felt a fool for not thinking of it sooner. He had been to Belle's flat with me several times, and spent six weeks there when I was away. It made sense that he would have come here. But how on earth had he got here? It must be a mile and a half from our pitch at the Angel. Had he walked all the way? If so, how long had he been here?

None of that mattered now. As I carried on making a fuss of him, he licked my hand, his tongue was as rough as sandpaper. He rubbed his face against mine and curled his tail.

I rang Belle's doorbell and she invited me in. My mood had been transformed from despair to delirium. I was on top of the world

Belle's flatmate was also there and said, 'Want something to celebrate?' smiling, knowingly.

'No, I'm fine thanks,' I said, tugging on Bob as he scratched playfully at my hand, and looking over at Belle. 'Just a beer would be great.'

Bob didn't need drugs to get through the night. He just needed his companion: me. And at that moment I decided that was all I needed too. All I needed was Bob. Not just tonight, but for as long as I had the privilege of having him in my life.

21

Bob, The *Big Issue* Cat

As the March sun disappeared and dusk descended over the Angel, London was winding itself up for the evening once more. The traffic was already thick on Islington High Street and the honking of horns was building into a cacophony of noise. The pavements were busy too, with a stream of people flowing in and out of the station concourse. The rush hour was under way and living up to its name as usual. Everyone was in a rush to get somewhere it seemed. Well, not quite everyone.

I was checking that I had enough papers left to cope with the surge of activity I knew was about to arrive when I saw out of the corner of my eye that a group of kids had gathered around us. They were teenagers I guessed, three boys and a couple of girls. They looked South American or maybe Spanish or Portuguese.

There was nothing unusual about this. It wasn't quite Covent Garden, Leicester Square or Piccadilly Circus, but Islington had its fair share of tourists and Bob was a magnet for them. Barely a day went by without him being surrounded by an excitable group of youths like this.

What was different this evening, however, was the way they were animatedly pointing and talking about him.

'Ah, *si* Bob,' said one teenage girl, talking what

I guessed was Spanish.

'*Si, si.* Bob the Beeg Issew Cat,' said another.

Weird, I thought to myself when I realised what she'd said. *How do they know his name is Bob? He doesn't wear a name tag. And what do they mean by the* Big Issue *Cat?*

My curiosity soon got the better of me.

'Sorry, I hope you don't mind me asking, but how do you know Bob?' I said, in the hope that one of them spoke decent English. My Spanish was almost non-existent.

Fortunately one of them, a young boy, replied. 'Oh, we see him on YouTube,' he smiled. 'Bob is very popular, yes?'

'Is he?' I said. 'Someone told me he was on YouTube, but I've got no idea how many people watch it.'

'Many people, I think,' he smiled.

'Where are you from?'

'*España,* Spain.'

'So Bob's popular in Spain?'

'*Si, si,*' another one of the boys said when the boy translated back our conversation. '*Bob es una estrella en España.*'

'Sorry, what did he say?' I asked the boy.

'He says that Bob is a star in Spain.'

I was shocked.

I knew that lots of people had taken photographs of Bob over the years, both while I was busking and now that I was selling the *Big Issue.* I'd jokingly wondered once whether he should be put forward for the *Guinness Book of Records*: the world's most photographed cat.

A couple of people had filmed him too, some

243

with their phones, others with proper video cameras. I started casting my mind back over those that had shot footage of him in recent months. Who could have shot a film that was now on YouTube? There were a couple of obvious candidates, but I made a note to check it out at the first opportunity.

The following morning I headed down to the local library with Bob and booked myself online.

I punched in the search terms: Bob Big Issue Cat. Sure enough, there was a link to YouTube, which I clicked on. To my surprise there was not one, but two films there.

'Hey Bob, look, he was right. You are a star on YouTube.'

He hadn't been terribly interested until that point. It wasn't Channel Four racing, after all. But when I clicked on the first video and saw and heard myself talking he jumped on to the keyboard and popped his face right up against the screen.

As I watched the first film, which was called 'Bobcat and I', the memory came back to me. I'd been approached by a film student. He'd followed me around for a while back during the days when we were selling the *Big Issue* around Neal Street. There was nice footage of us there and of us getting on the bus and walking the streets. Watching the film it gave a pretty good summary of the day-to-day life of a *Big Issue* seller. There were clips of people fussing over Bob, but also a sequence where I was confronted by some guys who didn't believe he was a 'tame' cat. They belonged to the same group of people who thought I was drugging him.

The other video had been filmed more recently around the Angel by a Russian guy. I clicked on the link for that and saw that he'd called his film 'Bob The *Big Issue* Cat'. This must have been the one that the Spanish students had seen. I could see that it had had tens of thousands of hits. I was gobsmacked.

The feeling that Bob was becoming some kind of celebrity had been building for a while. Every now and again someone would say: 'Ah, is that Bob? I've heard about him.' Or 'Is this the famous Bobcat?' I'd always assumed it was through word of mouth. Then, a few weeks before meeting the Spanish teenagers, we had featured in a local newspaper, the *Islington Tribune*. I'd even been approached by an American lady, an agent, who asked me whether I'd thought about writing a book about me and Bob. As if!

The Spanish teenagers made me realise that it had begun to morph into something much more than local celebrity. Bob was becoming a feline star.

★　★　★

As I headed towards the bus stop and absorbed what I had just discovered, I couldn't help smiling. On one of the films I had said that Bob had saved my life. When I first heard it I thought it sounded a bit crass, a bit of an exaggeration too. But as I walked along the road and put it all into perspective it began to sink in: it was true, he really had.

In the two years since I'd found him sitting in that half-lit hallway, he had transformed my world. Back then I'd been a recovering heroin addict living a hand-to-mouth existence. I was in my late twenties and yet I had no real direction or purpose in life beyond survival. I'd lost contact with my family and barely had a friend in the world. Not to put too fine a point on it, my life was a total mess. All that had changed.

My trip to Australia hadn't made up for the difficulties of the past, but it had brought me and my mother back together again. The wounds were being healed. I had the feeling we were going to become close again. My battle with drugs was finally drawing to a close, or at least, I hoped it was. The amount of Subutex I had to take was diminishing steadily. The day when I wouldn't have to take it all was looming into view on the horizon. I could finally see an end to my addiction. There had been times when I'd never imagined that was possible.

Most of all, I'd finally laid down some roots. It might not have seemed much to most people, but my little flat in Tottenham had given me the kind of security and stability that I'd always secretly craved. I'd never lived for so long in the same place: I'd been there more than four years and would remain there even longer. There was no doubt in my mind that would not have happened if it hadn't been for Bob.

I was raised as a churchgoer but I wasn't a practising Christian. I wasn't an agnostic or atheist either. My view is that we should all take a bit from every religion and philosophy. I'm not

246

a Buddhist but I like Buddhist philosophies, in particular. They give you a very good structure that you can build your life around. For instance, I definitely believe in karma, the idea that what goes around, comes around. I wondered whether Bob was my reward for having done something good, somewhere in my troubled life.

I also wondered sometimes whether Bob and I had known each other in a previous life. The way we bonded together, the instant connection that we made, that was very unusual. Someone said to me once that we were the reincarnation of Dick Whittington and his cat. Except the roles had been reversed this time around, Dick Whittington had come back as Bob — and I was his companion. I didn't have a problem with that. I was happy to think of him in that way. Bob is my best mate and the one who has guided me towards a different — and a better — way of life. He doesn't demand anything complicated or unrealistic in return. He just needs me to take care of him. And that's what I do.

I knew the road ahead wouldn't be smooth. We were sure to face our problems here and there — I was still working on the streets of London, after all. It was never going to be easy. But as long as we were together, I had a feeling it was going to be fine.

Everybody needs a break, everybody deserves that second chance. Bob and I had taken ours . . .

Acknowledgements

Writing this book has been an amazing collaborative experience, one in which so many people have played their part.

First and foremost I'd like to thank my family, and my mum and dad in particular, for giving me the sheer bloody-minded determination that has kept me going through some dark times in my life. I'd also like to thank my godparents, Terry and Merilyn Winters, for being such great friends to me.

On the streets of London, so many people have shown kindness to me over the years, but I'd like to single out Sam, Tom, Lee and Rita, the *Big Issue* co-ordinators who have been so generous to me. I'd also like to thank outreach workers Kevin and Chris for their compassion and understanding. Thanks also the Blue Cross and RSPCA for their valuable advice and Davika, Leanne and the rest of the staff at Angel tube station who have been so supportive of me and Bob.

I'd also like to thank Food For Thought and Pix in Neal Street who have always offered me and Bob a warm cup of tea and a saucer of milk, as well as Daryl at Diamond Jacks in Soho and Paul and Den the cobblers who have always been my good friends. I'd like also to mention Pete Watkins at Corrupt Drive Records, DJ Cavey Nik at Mosaic Homes and Ron Richardson.

* ★ ★

This book would never have happened if it hadn't been for my agent Mary Pachnos. It was she who first approached me with the idea. It sounded pretty crazy at the time, and I'd never have been able to get it all down and turned into a coherent story without the help of her and the writer Garry Jenkins. So a heartfelt thanks to both Mary and Garry. At my publishers, Hodder & Stoughton, I'd like to thank Rowena Webb, Ciara Foley, Emma Knight and the rest of the brilliant team there. Thanks also to Alan and the staff at Waterstone's in Islington who even let me and Garry work on the book in the quiet upstairs. And a big thank you to Kitty, who without her constant support we'd both be lost.

Finally I'd like to thank Scott Hartford-Davis and the Dalai Lama who have, in recent years, given me a great philosophy by which to live my life, and Leigh Ann, who is in my thoughts.

★ ★ ★

Last, and most definitely not least, of course, I have to thank the little fellow who came into my life in 2007 and who — from the moment I befriended him — has proven to be such a positive, life-changing force in my life. Everyone deserves a friend like Bob. I have been very fortunate indeed to have found one . . .

James Bowen
London, January 2012

We do hope that you have enjoyed reading this large print book.

Did you know that all of our titles are available for purchase?

We publish a wide range of high quality large print books including:
Romances, Mysteries, Classics
General Fiction
Non Fiction and Westerns

Special interest titles available in large print are:
The Little Oxford Dictionary
Music Book
Song Book
Hymn Book
Service Book

Also available from us courtesy of Oxford University Press:
Young Readers' Dictionary
(large print edition)
Young Readers' Thesaurus
(large print edition)

For further information or a free brochure, please contact us at:
Ulverscroft Large Print Books Ltd.,
The Green, Bradgate Road, Anstey,
Leicester, LE7 7FU, England.
Tel: (00 44) 0116 236 4325
Fax: (00 44) 0116 234 0205

THE BABY LAUNDRY FOR UNMARRIED MOTHERS

Angela Patrick and Lynne Barrett-Lee

In 1963, Angela Brown was nineteen and enjoying her first job working in the City of London. But then, a brief fling with a charismatic charmer left her pregnant, unmarried and facing a stark future. Her strict Catholic parents forced her to leave her job and family, and sent her to a convent in Essex for her confinement. Run like a Victorian workhouse, the nuns there vilified Angela for her 'wickedness'. After a terrifying labour with no pain relief, Angela gave birth to a beautiful son, Paul. At eight weeks he was taken from her and forcibly put up for adoption. Heartbroken, Angela thought about him every single day. Then, thirty years later, a letter came. It was from Paul, and a reunion was arranged . . .

TAKE ME HOME

Tessa Cunningham

When Tessa Cunningham's ninety-five-year-old father fell and broke his hip, a care home seemed the best option. But visiting him one day, Tessa saw in his eyes the yearning he was too proud to articulate: Please take me home. Tessa had just recovered from breast cancer, was in the throes of getting divorced and her daughters were soon to leave home. Yet she found herself moving her dad in, along with his zimmer frame, collection of hearing aid batteries and tins of Black Bullets mints. And in the months that followed, his unexpected wisdom and irrepressible ebullience helped to heal Tessa's pain.

HOME TO ROOST

Tessa Hainsworth

After two years, Tessa Hainsworth is no longer the outsider from London. She's finally become accepted into her tight-knit Cornish village community. But everyday life for Tessa is not like the holiday posters. Incomers to the village must tread carefully — if they don't, the village soon lets them know and Tessa finds herself torn between old friends and new. Still struggling to make ends meet, she rents out her home to summer holidaymakers — and helps run a B&B — with hilarious results. Tessa's job as a postwoman involves being an amateur health-and-safety inspector, a shoulder to cry on and a matchmaker, but there's always time for a sandwich in the sun and a bit of beachcombing in her lunch break.

THREE WISHES

Carey Goldberg, Beth Jones and Pamela Ferdinand

After chasing headlines from Manhattan to Moscow, Carey is the first of three friends to abandon the traditional path to motherhood. Finding the perfect anonymous donor, she buys eight vials of his sperm. But on the day the vials arrive, she meets a man online. They fall in love. And she gets pregnant the old-fashioned way. Carey passes the vials to Beth, who is recently divorced. But before she can use the vials, Beth meets a man on an ice-climbing trip. She too falls in love. And gets pregnant. So she gives the vials to Pam, an eternal romantic, who will never stop searching for the love of her life, but is ready to be a single mother. Then the magic strikes again . . .